PUNCH
PILLOW CRAFT

PUNCH
PILLOW CRAFT

by Nan Orshefsky

BOBBS-MERRILL

Indianapolis/New York

Published by The Bobbs-Merrill Company, Inc.
Indianapolis / New York

Library of Congress Cataloging in Publication Data
Orshefsky, Nan.
Punch pillow craft.
1. Pillows. 2. Punched work. I. Title.
TT410.O77   746.4′4   76-10084
ISBN 0-672-52126-1

Designed by Beri Greenwald
Manufactured in the United States of America

First printing

For my mother, Ruth Taylor Day

CONTENTS

PUNCH
PILLOW CRAFT

INTRODUCTION

I CALL THESE PILLOWS Punch Pillows because they are made with a rug punch needle which is simply punched through a piece of burlap.

The first pillows I made were modeled on members of my own family. They were punch pillows made to be punched. I figured that if I made pillows of my three children, they could take out their sibling rivalries on the stuffed versions, thereby saving wear and tear on the originals. It didn't work out quite that way—the pillow children proved too appealing. Instead of punching it, I found my two daughters hugging and kissing the pillow portrait of their brother. And while their own pillows sweetly shared the couch, the two of them had at each other on the floor.

No matter. My younger daughter, then in second grade, decided that her pillow image needed a friend. She borrowed my punch needle and made another little girl pillow dressed in a nightgown because, she explained, "She's come for a sleep-over."

The family grew. Father was added—he's the only pillow person lying down because he's taking a nap. Cousins, aunts and uncles joined the people pillows, followed by dogs, cats and birds. Next, the garden blossomed with daisy pillows. Butterflies and snails appeared. Fish began to swim across the couch and monsters to share the beds. Finally, the whole house and a barn developed on a bolster.

In designing this book, I've tried to keep the family flexible. Its members can be adapted to resemble the members of your family or friends by changing the color of their yarn hair or eye buttons, or by altering their style of dress. Variations are suggested with most of the designs, and they are meant to suggest the many other variations that are possible as well.

Punch pillows are very easy to make. The actual punching involves pushing the needle

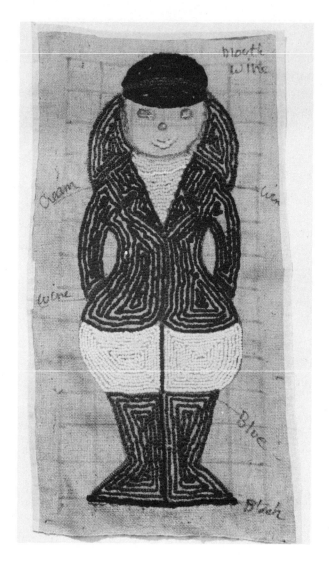

through the burlap, withdrawing it carefully and pushing it through again. Each punch leaves a yarn loop on the reverse side of the burlap. There is no fancy cutting, knotting or complicated stitching to master. Varying the length of the loops gives the work interesting sculptured effects. The photos will give you an idea of what it will look like from the front and also from the back (before you add backing to it). And to get this effect, all it takes is a little wire gauge that comes with the punch needle. Because the loops are shaggy and the yarn is thick, minor mistakes disappear into the total mass and seldom show when the work is finished. If a mistake is more than minor, it's easy to pull it out, push the weave of the burlap together again and punch it over.

Punching is fast work. Once you get the rhythm, the loops multiply very quickly. And when you've finished punching the design, turning it into a pillow doesn't take long, either. There's no need for professional blocking—iron-on interfacing keeps the loops from pulling out. Sewing on the pillow backing is a simple operation that can be done by hand or machine. Stuffing the pillow is even simpler. It's possible to finish a punch pillow completely in just a day or two.

In addition to being easy to make and fast, punch pillows cost very little. Unlike other hobbies that require expensive equipment, all you need to get started is a number 6 rug punch needle which costs less than a dollar, a piece of burlap and some rug-and-craft yarn. A sturdy cotton remnant can serve as the pillow backing, and the other minor supplies you'll need, such as masking tape and a couple of heavy duty felt markers, are probably in your work drawer already.

All the designs given here are drawn on simple grids so that they can be transferred easily from the book to your burlap. In most cases, the instructions for punching a particular design are given in terms of color. You may find it easier or less tedious to change the order in which you punch the design. There's no reason not to, although as a general rule it's advisable to punch the light colors last so they won't become soiled while you're working on the rest of the pillow. I've tried to make the color directions as clear as possible. However, if you're ever in doubt, check the color photograph to verify the color of the part of the design you're working on.

Punch pillows are fun to make. Anyone can enjoy punching them—male or female, young or old. If you've never done anything like this before, start out by choosing one of the simplest designs—the triangle or the large daisy, or the mouse or the cat. Then move on to a slightly more complicated one.

Once you've learned the technique, you can invent your own punch pillows. Everyone has a punch pillow just waiting to be punched. I hope the designs I've included here will inspire you to create a hand-crafted, made-to-order punch pillow world of your own.

PART

Before You Begin

CHAPTER

1

MATERIALS

THE BASIC INGREDIENTS for making a punch pillow are a piece of burlap, a punch needle and an assortment of yarns. You'll also need a few other inexpensive supplies, but let's talk about the three basics first.

THE BURLAP

By far the most satisfactory base that I have found for punch pillows is plain, unassuming burlap. It has the weave to hold the punch loops and enough body to be used without a frame. Burlap has an interesting texture if parts of the pattern are left bare, and it comes in a wide range of colors as well as in natural. Natural burlap has the added advantage of being washable (colored burlap is not). Rug shampoo is best for soiled pillows.

Where To Find It

You can find good burlap in decorator colors in the home-furnishings section of most department stores. For natural-colored burlap, try your nearest garden center, where it's sold to shield delicate shrubs and trees from the rigors of winter. Garden center burlap may not be quite as refined as the department store variety, but chances are the price will be a good deal lower, and it serves the purpose just as well, if it is good quality with a tight weave.

A look through the yellow pages of the telephone book under the listing "burlap" will provide names and addresses of more specialized sources of supply.

What to Look for and How Much to Buy

Wherever you buy it, look for a piece of burlap with a good even weave, the tighter the better. A few flaws won't matter if they are small ones.

Burlap is sold by the yard. It varies in width, especially at garden centers. One yard is enough for several pillows—the exact number depending, of course, on the width of the burlap and the size of the pillows you plan to make.

THE PUNCH NEEDLE

All the pillows in this book were made with a number 6 rug punch needle. It is a very simple tool, costs less than a dollar, and comes with a wire gauge that allows you to make short loops as well as long ones. It's available at most variety stores, department stores and craft centers.

THE YARN

You need heavy rug-and-craft yarn for making punch pillows. There are several different kinds and their composition varies, but any one will do if it is heavy enough. There's no need to confine yourself to using just one type of yarn any more than you need limit yourself as to color. Actually, your punch pillows can be even more attractive if you combine different types of yarn, for the contrast in textures, like a contrast in colors, adds interest to the final result. Just be sure that, whatever yarn you buy, you buy *continuous skeins*—don't buy the pre-cut yarn that's used for making hooked rugs.

Kinds

A rayon-and-cotton mixture is the commonest and least expensive yarn you can buy. It is usually packaged in 70-yard skeins and comes in the widest range of colors.

One hundred percent acrylic rug yarn is slightly fuzzier and shinier than the rayon-and-cotton mixture. It usually comes in skeins of 140 yards.

Orlon rug-and-craft yarn is softer than either of the other two and somewhat easier to work with. Like the acrylic, it, too, usually comes in 140-yard skeins.

Regular knitting worsted is not bulky enough by itself to be used in the number 6 rug punch needle. However, you can use it by doubling it. To do this, use two separate balls of yarn, take the end of each and thread them together through the punch needle. You can use two strands of the same color, or one strand each of two different colors for a tweedy effect. You can combine knitting worsted with regular rug yarn in the same way, by threading one strand of each through the needle. But be sure that the two strands together are not too bulky—*the yarn must be able to move through the needle freely at all times.*

Colors

Rug-and-craft yarns come in a wide range of exciting colors. And because it's perfectly all right to use different types of yarn in the same design, you can choose from them all the colors that please you most. If you find a vibrant orange in acrylic, a good green in orlon and a sunny yellow in a rayon-and-cotton yarn, don't hesitate to buy all three of them even though they're different kinds of yarn. Just make sure you buy enough yarn in each color to complete your pillow. Color lots vary, and you may never find exactly the same shade again if you run out.

I have suggested specific colors to use with each of the designs in this book, and I've tried to give the names that best describe the colors I used. But color names vary. Manufacturers can't seem to get together on them. A yarn called "spring green" by one company may look just like one called "chartreuse" or "lime" by another. Even when a color has a sim-

ple name, such as "yellow," it can vary greatly, depending on the brand. You'll find the names don't mean a thing unless you have the yarn in hand. Use the color photographs in the book for a double check.

Most of the patterns given here use less than a full skein of any particular color. Save your leftovers. As you continue to punch different designs, you'll build up a reserve of colors you'll be able to draw on for the future pillows you punch, just as an artist draws on his palette of paints.

Getting the Yarn Ready to Use

Some rug-and-craft yarns come in pull-out skeins, ready to use. If the yarn you choose is not packaged in a pull-out skein, you'll have to wind it into workable balls. To do this, loop the yarn over the backs of two chairs, find an end and start winding loosely around your fingers. Make each skein into four or five separate balls—these small balls are easier to work with once you start punching.

Where to Find It and How Much to Buy

Rug yarn is available in most variety stores, department stores and craft centers. Specialized craft shops are a superior source for heavy yarns in all colors.

I have given the amounts of yarn you will need with each pattern. However, it is difficult to figure exact amounts. As a general rule, the bulkier the yarn, the less you will require. Ten yards of a fat orlon will easily fill an area that would take fifteen yards of a lighter weight acrylic. Rug yarns often vary in bulk, too, depending on the brand. And people vary in their punching—some people punch tighter stitches than others, which means that the amount of yarn they use will be more in the long run.

As a general gauge, you can count on needing about four yards of yarn to fill a two-inch square with the long loop, and about three yards to fill a two-inch square with the short loop. If you are punching in a straight line, one yard of yarn will go about four to five inches in the long loop, and about seven to eight inches in the short loop.

Because of the many variables, all the yarn measurements I have given with each pattern are approximate. But I have tried to be generous with my approximations so that you won't run short.

ADDITIONAL SUPPLIES

You will need a few other supplies for your punch pillow in addition to the burlap, the punch needle and yarn. You'll need material for backing your pillow, filler for stuffing it, and a few simple items of trim for some of the designs. These are all listed at the beginning of each design, along with the dimensions of the burlap and backing material required for that particular pillow.

When you have finished punching the design and are ready to finish your pillow, you'll find the information you need to complete it in Part III. Meanwhile, you'll find it easier to proceed if you assemble the following items together before you settle down to begin:

- a pair of scissors
- a rule or yardstick (you can often obtain a yardstick free from a local paint store or lumberyard)
- a roll of masking tape
- 2 heavy duty permanent felt markers (I prefer blue and black; however, you can use any two colors provided they show up on the burlap and are easily distinguished from each other)
- a knitting needle and a crochet hook to even up irregular loops

CHAPTER

2

GETTING YOUR DESIGN ONTO THE BURLAP

FOR ALL THE PILLOWS in this book, the procedure is the same. Here is how you start.

PREPARING THE BURLAP

Measuring and Cutting

If the burlap is badly creased or wrinkled, iron it first so that it will lie flat and be easier to work with. If it has been carelessly cut or has a frayed edge, look for the first thread that runs completely across the width of the material and draw it out gently. This will leave a ladder in the weave that can serve as a guide for you to cut a straight edge.

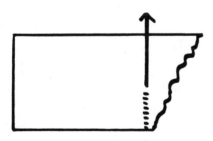

Taping the Edges

Measure the burlap with a yardstick or ruler, then cut it to the size called for by the design instructions. That size will always include an allowance for a two-inch margin all around, which is needed for taping the edges and for seaming the pillow at the finish.

Burlap frays easily, and frayed edges can give you problems when you're punching. You can avoid this by binding the edges with masking tape.

As soon as you have cut a piece of burlap to the size you need, place a piece of masking tape along one edge so that you can bend half the width of the tape over the edge to seal it. Do this along each edge

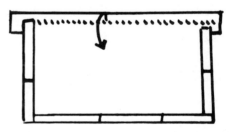

except the selvage, which won't fray and so doesn't need to be taped. If you have a long edge to bind, don't try to do it with one stretch of tape—chances are you'll get more stuck onto your fingers or the tape itself than onto the burlap. Cut the tape into manageable lengths and apply each strip separately until you have bound all the cut edges.

DRAWING THE GRID

All the designs in this book were worked out on a grid so that they can be transferred easily to a grid drawn on your burlap. The grid is always drawn on the wrong side so it will not be visible on the finished pillow. With the exception of the bolsters, the grid for each design is made up of two-inch squares. The total number of squares may vary, but the principle is the same in every case.

Take your taped piece of burlap and secure it to the table, floor or other surface you are working on with a little piece of masking tape at each corner to prevent it from slipping. Now take your ruler or yardstick. Using your blue felt marker, draw the outline of the grid two inches in from the taped edges on all four sides. Mark each line at two-inch intervals as you complete it. Connect these marks by drawing vertical and horizontal lines to complete the interior of the grid. Check to make sure you have the proper number of squares for the height and width of the design you've chosen.

TRANSFERRING THE DESIGN

The Centerline

Most of the designs have a centerline. I found, when drawing free hand, that I invariably make the right side bigger than the left. Some of my early punch pillow people had very large right feet and lopsided stomachs. Once I started using a grid with a centerline, these distortions disappeared. The centerline is useful for checking to see that the right and left sides of your drawing are equal. It's also useful to help you locate key points in the design, which make it easier for you to transfer it.

Locating the Key Points

Instructions with each pillow list key points of the design. A key point may be a nose that will help you place the eyes and the mouth, a belt that will indicate the center of a figure, or the fin of a fish that will help you locate the body outline. Look for these key points on the design in the book, and transfer them to the same grid location on your burlap, using your blue felt marker. They will be your guideposts for transferring the complete design.

The Preliminary Drawing

Starting from the key points and working outward, square by square, copy the design from the book grid onto the grid on your burlap. Draw it in lightly with your blue felt marker. Check your drawing against the book and correct any mistakes.

Often a line will curve through several squares. Draw it tentatively and go over it until it looks right.

Making the Final Pattern

Note that the book design is drawn with a straight line for short loops and a wiggly line for long loops. Be sure to duplicate these lines in your final drawing.

〰〰〰〰〰〰〰 LONG LOOPS

▬▬▬▬▬▬▬ SHORT LOOPS

Using the heavy duty permanent black felt marker, go over all the blue lines of your preliminary sketch with a strong black line. By changing colors, your final pattern will stand out clearly against the grid and your preliminary drawing.

NUMBERING FOR COLORS

Colors in the designs are indicated by numbers. Each design has its own color scheme, so the same number doesn't refer to the same color in every case. If you are working on a big design and can't remember which number stands for which color, you can write the name of the color with a felt marker either in the area where it belongs, or in the margin, keyed to the area with an arrow.

It's easy to change the color scheme given for one of your own, if you prefer. Just remember to maintain the balance of colors necessary for the design to be effective. For example, if you want to replace a "red" with a "pink," use that same pink everywhere the red is indicated.

How to Make the Design Larger or Smaller

You can change the size of any of the designs easily by changing the size of the grid squares. If you want to make a giant belly dancer, for instance, make your grid squares larger—say, four inches instead of two. If you want to reduce the size—to make a smaller fish, for example—make your grid squares smaller, one-and-a-half instead of two inches.

A note of caution about reducing the size of a design: if a pillow gets too small, it will be difficult to punch the design, and the pillow itself may lose impact as a spot of color on the couch. Also, keep in mind that the amount of yarn you will need will change accordingly, if you change the size of a pillow.

VARIATIONS

Variations are given for many of the designs in the book, and there may be other changes you'd like to make in some of the pillows. Feel free to do so—just try to keep your changes simple. Remember, you'll be working on the pillow inside out, and you'll have to turn it right side out again when you stuff it, so you don't want a lot of complicated knobs or curlicues that will get in the way.

WORKING WITH A FRAME

You can attach the burlap to a frame if you think it will make it easier for you to work, although I don't consider it necessary for any of the designs here, with the possible exception of the bolsters. Large projects, such as a rug, require a frame, but for smaller ones, such as a pillow, a frame is op-

tional. I like the flexibility of being able to roll up the burlap with the yarn and the needle, stuff it into a bag, and take it with me to the dentist's office or on a picnic. However, young children with small hands may find it easier to hold the burlap if it is framed.

You can make a simple frame from slats of wood, $\frac{5}{8}'' \times 1\frac{1}{2}''$, cut to the length you need. Or you can use artists' canvas stretcher bars, which are sold in art supply stores. These come in all sizes, so you can buy them to fit together in the dimensions you need for any particular design. Stretcher bars are measured by their outside dimensions, so if you plan to use them as a frame, measure their inside dimensions and allow a little leeway between the inside of the frame and the edge of your design.

An old wooden window frame, if you happen to have one around, or a shallow wooden fruit crate can also be turned into a makeshift frame.

After your final design is on your burlap and you have numbered it for colors, tack or staple the burlap to your frame, leaving a generous margin.

CHAPTER

3

HOW TO USE THE PUNCH NEEDLE

THE NUMBER 6 rug punch needle, used for all the designs in this book, makes two kinds of loops—long and short. The variations in the length of the loops add texture, interest and a sculptured look to the pillows. The needle comes equipped with a removable wire gauge.

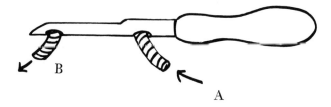

THREADING THE NEEDLE

It's easier to thread the needle if you remove the wire gauge first. But put it down where you'll be able to find it again easily—it's an unobtrusive little wire and can disappear quickly in a jumble of yarn and burlap.

Pass the end of the yarn from the outside through eye A at the base of the needle, along the groove in the shaft, then out through eye B at the point. Leave one inch of yarn protruding from the point.

Replace the wire gauge if you're going to punch short loops.

THE BASIC TECHNIQUE

Keep in mind that you are working from the "wrong" side of your pillow. The loops you punch will come out on the opposite side of the burlap, which will be the finished side. If you have never used a rug punch needle before, it might be wise to practice on a piece of scrap first, before starting on your design.

Where to Begin

Whenever you are beginning any section of a design, punch the outline first and then fill in.

Punching the Loops

The technique for punching both loops is exactly the same. The only difference is that you use the punch needle with the wire gauge for the short loops and without it for the long ones. With the gauge in place, the needle makes short loops, about ¼ inch long. Without the gauge, the needle makes long loops, about ⅜ to ½ inch long.

Whether you're making short loops or long ones, always push the needle through the burlap as far as it will go. The wire gauge will stop it halfway if you are punching short loops. If you are punching

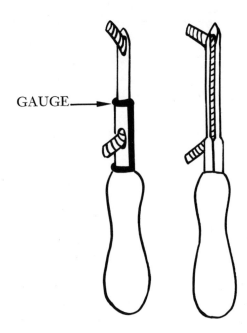

GAUGE —→

How to Start Punching

To start punching, hold the needle with the grooved side up, facing the direction in which you are working. Push the needle through the burlap as far as it will go. Pull the one inch of loose yarn pro-

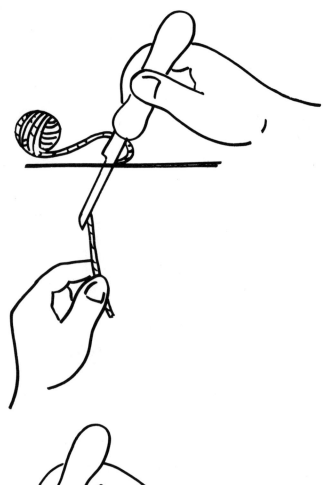

long loops, push the needle through to the hilt of the shaft before withdrawing the point.

Long loops are easier to make than short ones for a novice puncher. For one thing, they're made without the wire gauge, which can catch the yarn if you're not careful. For another, rows of long loops don't have to be as close together as rows of short loops. About four to five rows of long loops will fill an inch of your design, while it will take from five to six rows of short loops to fill the same area. (The actual count will depend on the character of the yarn you're using—the bulkier the yarn, the fewer stitches will be required.)

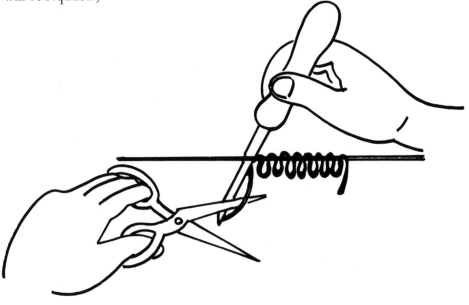

truding from the point out on the bottom or "right" side of the burlap.

Withdraw the point of the needle carefully to the surface of the burlap, but *do not lift the point of the needle off the surface*. Advance the needle slightly and punch through again. Keep your stitches close together—figure about five to six stitches per inch.

How to Stop Punching

When you reach the end of the piece of yarn you're working with, or you're ready to change colors, push the needle through the burlap to the right side and cut the yarn at eye B, near the point. Hold the end of the yarn with your left hand as you withdraw the needle to keep it from pulling through. Trim the yarn end so that it is even with the loops around it.

How to Fill In

Once you have the outline of an area punched, you can fill it in by punching in rows back and forth or up and down; or you can work in concentric circles going in toward the center.

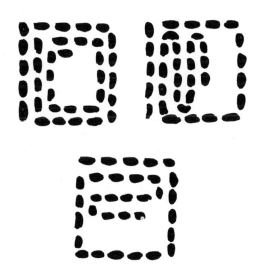

How to Work

Turn the burlap as you work, to keep the grooved side of the punch needle pointing in the direction in which you're going.

Keep the yarn slack. The yarn must be able to feed freely through the needle. Be careful not to put the heel of your hand on it while you're punching. Knitters beware that you don't automatically loop the yarn around your fingers. Anything that obstructs the flow of the yarn will cause the loops to pull out.

Watch the wire gauge. When the wire gauge is in place for short loops, be careful it doesn't catch or pinch the yarn as it feeds through the needle. Twist the gauge around on the needle until you get it into a position where it will not impede the yarn.

Check your work from time to time, by turning the burlap over to make sure your loops are even and to see how well you're progressing. Push the needle through the burlap before you turn it over so that you don't pull out any loops in the process.

Punch light areas last. If possible, when punching your design, save the light areas for last. White, light yellow, pink or any other light-colored yarn, if punched first, may get dingy while you're punching in the darker colors.

PROBLEMS AND WHAT TO DO ABOUT THEM

If the Loops Pull Out

There may be several reasons for this. Look through the list below to find the answer. But before you start to repunch the same area, always push the weave back together with your fingernail or the point of the needle. And don't punch in exactly the same holes the second time.

1. Check to make sure your yarn is slack. If it's too taut or is catching on the wire gauge, correct this and try again.

2. If the burlap is loosely woven, it may not hold the loops. You can remedy this by holding the burlap taut between the heel of your right hand and your left hand. Make your stitches close together; hold the needle perpendicular to the burlap to avoid leaving too much room between punches. If you have trouble holding the burlap taut, try using an embroidery hoop to frame the area you're punching.

3. If you are punching in a straight line, you may be putting too much strain on a few threads of the burlap. Try jumping a thread or two to the side with each stitch, alternating from left to right. By jumping back and forth this way you can tighten

the weave as you go and still proceed in the same direction.

4. If you hit a really swampy area in the burlap, change the direction in which you're going. Go back the way you came, make a circle and sneak up on it from the other side. The more loops you punch, the tighter the weave will become.

5. If your stitches still pull out, hold the loop on the bottom side of the burlap with the middle finger of your left hand. But don't hold the loop until you have withdrawn the point of the needle and are ready for the next punch. If you hold it too soon, the loop will be too long (see Extra Long Loops on page 28).

If the Loops Are Uneven

1. If the irregularities are minor, don't worry about them. Slight discrepancies disappear into the total mass of loops when the pillow is finished.

2. If you miss a couple of loops in a row, you can jump over and fill them in the next time you come around.

3. A knitting needle is a handy tool for evening up a row of irregular loops. Slip the knitting needle through the loops and pull it up until they're even.

4. A crochet hook can be used to pull up an individual loop to match the height of the other loops around it.

5. When you have finished punching the design, the weave of the burlap will have tightened. You can go back then over skimpy areas and fill them in with extra punches of the proper loops. This will

both hide bare spots and strengthen the lines of the design. It's the way to correct weak areas in general.

Starting Over

If the stitches look hopeless and there are just too many bald spots to repair with the remedies suggested above, pull out the whole area and start over again. Give the yarn a tug on the back side and it will pull out in a jiffy. You can use the same yarn again—just remember not to punch in exactly the same holes.

If you decide you don't like a particular color you've punched, use the same technique and change the yarn. To turn a blonde into a brunette, snatch her bald, push the weave together and punch her hair in a darker color yarn.

OTHER TYPES OF LOOPS

Once you have mastered the standard long loop and short loop, you are ready for a few variations.

Extra Long Loops

For whiskers and other special effects. Start out as you would for a long loop, punching the needle through the burlap as far as it will go. Then hold the loop with the fingers of your left hand as you withdraw the needle, letting the needle slide back along the yarn until the point emerges on the surface of the burlap. The result will be a loop twice as long as the standard long loop.

You can control the length of the loop and make a slightly shorter extra long loop by holding the yarn in this way with your left hand. If you want to make a series of loops this length, mark the shaft of the punch needle at the halfway point with nail polish or a felt marker. When you see the mark emerge, take hold of the loop. You can punch two or three different sizes of extra long loops this way, by marking the needle at different points on the shaft with different colors.

Extra Short Loops

For mouths, chins and other areas that you want to define with a flat stitch. To make these, turn the burlap over and work from the right side. This will give you the flat stitch that you see on the back when you're working standard loops. Use the short loop when you are working this way. Since the loops will appear on the back where the pattern is drawn, you may prefer to wait until you have finished punching the rest of the pattern before making these extra short stitches. Otherwise the loops may interfere with your punching.

Haphazard Loops

Use these to break up any large areas of solid color and to vary hair color.

First fill the area in which you plan to use them loosely with short or long loops, about four to five rows per inch. Then change your yarn color and punch through with the second color in a random fashion. Use long loops—they're less likely to pull out than short ones while you're jumping your needle around. And don't jump too far for each stitch. The length of your stitch is the same; only the direction you take is haphazard.

PART

The Pillows

A SAMPLING IN COLOR
FROM EACH SECTION

CHAPTER

4

SAMPLERS

Samplers provide an easy introduction to making punch pillows. A simple geometric design, based on a square, a triangle or a circle, offers you a chance to practice making both long and short loops. And when you're done you have an attractive pillow.

The triangle included in this chapter is so simple you can draw it directly on your burlap if you choose, using only a ruler, without bothering to draw a grid. Still, it might be a good idea for you to draw it on a grid for practice. You'll need a grid in any case for the two designs that follow the triangle, as well as for the somewhat more complicated people and animal pillows further on.

The instructions for each sampler include a list of all the materials you'll need both for punching the design and finishing the pillow. You'll find instructions for finishing your pillows in Chapter 12.

The Triangle

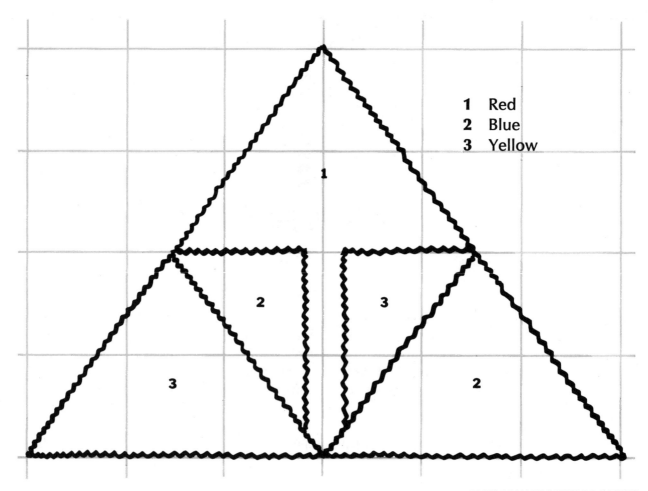

1 Red
2 Blue
3 Yellow

EACH SQUARE EQUALS 2 INCHES

MATERIALS

Burlap: 12″ × 16″; or triangular scrap, 16″ × 14″ × 14″ (tape the edges)
Yarn: red, 20 yards
      blue, 20 yards
      yellow, 20 yards

FOR FINISHING

Iron-on interfacing: 10″ × 14″; or triangular scrap, 14″ × 12″ × 12″
Backing: 12″ × 16″; or triangular scrap, 16″ × 14″ × 14″
Stuffing: ¼ pound polyester fiber

TRANSFERRING THE DESIGN

The base of the triangular pillow is broader than the sides. If you prefer to transfer the design directly onto your burlap without drawing a grid, use a ruler and your blue felt marker and draw the base of the triangle 12 inches straight across. From the midpoint of your base, measure 8 inches straight up. Then draw the two sides of the triangle, 10 inches each, to meet at that center point. Be sure to leave at least a 2-inch margin on all sides. Copy the rest of the design from the illustration. Check it for accuracy, then go over the drawing with your black felt marker.

If you want to use a grid, leave a 2-inch margin on all sides of your 12″ × 16″ piece of burlap and draw a grid of 2-inch squares, 6 squares wide by 4 squares high, with your blue felt marker. Find the center point on the top of your grid and use a ruler to connect it to the two corners of the grid base. Copy the rest of the design, square by square, from the illustration. Go over the final drawing with your black felt marker.

PUNCHING THE DESIGN

Red (1) *Long loop:* Starting at the top, outline the arrow-shaped area completely. Then fill in.

Blue (2) *Long loop:* Outline the triangle at the bottom right, then fill in. *Short loop:* Fill in the left center triangle (now partly outlined in long loop red).

Yellow (3) *Long loop:* Outline and fill in the triangle on the bottom left. *Short loop:* Fill in the right center triangle.

Check for any skimpy spots and fill in if necessary.

See Chapter 12 for instructions for finishing your pillow.

VARIATIONS

There are many ways you can vary this pillow. A simple one is to turn the top area into a triangle by using a fourth color for the strip in the center. If you do this, you'll need approximately 15 yards of each of the four colors. Do the center strip in long loop, and repeat the color in short loop in a single row around the outside of the entire triangle.

The Large Daisy

MATERIALS

Burlap: 16″ × 16″ (tape the edges)
Yarn: yellow orange, 15 yards
    rust, 15 yards
    red orange, 20 yards
    navy blue, 30 yards

FOR FINISHING

Iron-on interfacing: 14″ × 14″
Backing: 16″ × 16″
Stuffing: ⅓ pound polyester fiber

TRANSFERRING THE DESIGN

Leave a 2-inch margin on all sides and draw a grid of 2-inch squares, 6 squares wide by 6 squares high, with your blue felt marker. To make the outside circle of the daisy on your grid, use a compass set at 6 inches, or place a 12-inch plate on the center of your grid and draw around it. Locate the center of the flower and the four large petals as key points on your grid. Copy the rest of the design, square by square, from the illustration. Go over the finished drawing with your black felt marker.

PUNCHING THE DESIGN

Yellow orange (1) *Short loop:* Outline the two large horizontal petals, then fill in.

Rust (2) *Short loop:* Outline the two large vertical petals, then fill in.

Red orange (3) *Long loop:* Outline the four small petals between the large petals, then fill in. Outline and fill in the inside center of the flower. Punch one row to make the inner outside circle of the daisy.

Navy blue (4) *Long loop:* Fill in the outer center of the daisy. Fill in the entire background area around the flower up to the red orange outer circle. Punch one row all around just outside the outer red orange circle.

Check for any skimpy spots, especially in the outside circles, and fill in if necessary.

See Chapter 12 for instructions for finishing your pillow.

VARIATIONS

This simple flower pattern is easy to adapt to a color scheme of your own. Choose any four colors you like, but try to use bright colors in the petals and a darker color for the background and the outer inside circle in the center of the daisy.

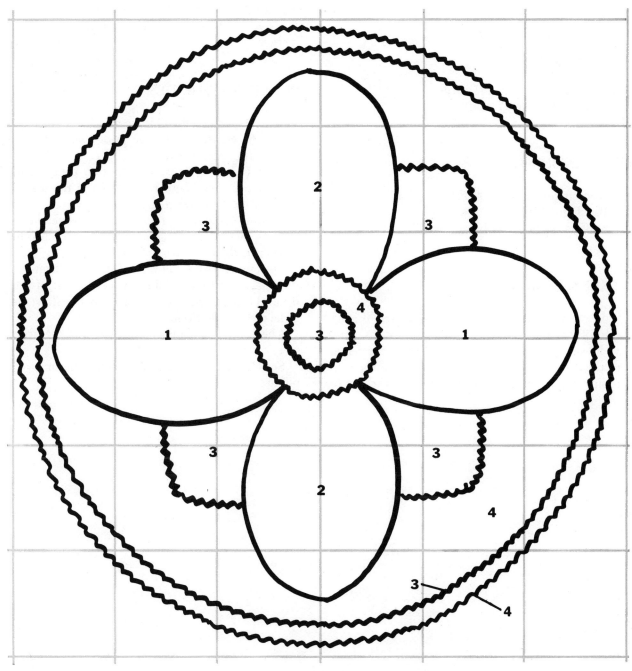

EACH SQUARE EQUALS 2 INCHES

1 Yellow orange
2 Rust
3 Red orange
4 Navy blue

The Small Daisy

MATERIALS

Burlap: red, 12″ × 12″ (tape the edges)
Yarn: red, 15 yards
    rust, 15 yards
    yellow orange, 15 yards
    dark olive, 17 yards

FOR FINISHING

Iron-on interfacing: 10″ × 10″
Backing: 12″ × 12″
Stuffing: ¼ pound polyester fiber

TRANSFERRING THE DESIGN

Leave a 2-inch margin on all sides and draw a grid of 2-inch squares, 4 squares high by 4 squares wide, with your blue felt marker. Locate the center of the daisy and the two vertical petals on the centerline as key points on your grid. Copy the rest of the design, square by square, from the illustration. Go over the final drawing with your black felt marker.

PUNCHING THE DESIGN

Red (1) *Long loop:* Outline the two vertical petals on the centerline of your grid. Then fill in the outer part of each petal.

Rust (2) *Long loop:* Outline two petals diagonally opposite each other, as shown in the illustration. Fill in the outer part of each petal.

Yellow orange (3) *Long loop:* Outline the remaining two petals diagonally opposite each other and fill in the outer part of each petal.

Dark olive (4) *Long loop:* Fill in the center of the daisy. *Short loop:* Fill in the center part of each petal. Then punch one row around the flower to make the outside circle.

Check for any skimpy spots and fill in if necessary.

See Chapter 12 for instructions for finishing your pillow.

EACH SQUARE EQUALS 2 INCHES

1 Red
2 Rust
3 Yellow orange
4 Dark olive

CHAPTER

5

THE PEOPLE PILLOWS

The punch pillow family assembled here is large and diverse. It includes two mothers, one father, one big brother, two big sisters, one little brother, a baby, dapper Uncle Dudley and Aunt Bella, the belly dancer.

All of the pillows were punched on natural burlap except where it's specified otherwise. Variations are given for most of the designs, but you can adapt any of the characters in any way you like to make them resemble members of your own family. You can choose a colored burlap that brings the complexion color closer to the character you have in mind—Uncle Dudley's

pink burlap suggests his slightly high blood pressure, for example, and Father's gold burlap reflects the tan he acquired while sleeping in the sun. You can vary the measurements—widen a waistline or add to the height or the size of the feet. Or you can change a hair style as well as its color, and the style and colors in which a character is dressed.

Feel free to make whatever changes you choose. But try to keep your design simple and to balance your colors to achieve an effective total look.

Mother I

MATERIALS

Burlap: 20″ × 30″ (tape the edges)
Yarn: bright gold, 40 yards
     pale gold, 65 yards
     wine, 65 yards·
     rust, 20 yards
     fuschia, 30 yards

TRIM

2 eye buttons
1 pink nose button

FOR FINISHING

Iron-on interfacing: 18″ × 28″
Backing: 20″ × 30″
Stuffing: 1¼ pounds polyester fiber

TRANSFERRING THE DESIGN

This is an easy design to transfer—much of it can be drawn on your grid with a ruler.

Leave a 2-inch margin on all sides and draw a grid of 2-inch squares, 8 squares wide by 13 squares high, with your blue felt marker.

Locate the nose, elbows and hands as key points on your grid. You can use a ruler to draw most of the lines of the body and the arms, but be sure you check carefully against the illustration so that your lines begin and end in the proper squares. Copy the rest of the design, square by square, from the illustration. Check against the centerline to make sure the sides are equal. Then go over the final drawing with your black felt marker.

PUNCHING THE DESIGN

Wine (3) *Long loop:* Outline and fill in the two large triangles at the bottom of the skirt. Punch the eyelashes. (The eye buttons will be added later as "trim.") *Short loop:* Outline and fill in the top of the dress above and below the arms.

Fuschia (5) *Long loop:* Outline and fill in the large triangle in the center of the skirt. *Short loop:* Outline and fill in the upper part of the sleeves. Turn your burlap over. Working from the front, punch the line of the mouth. Cut the yarn on the back.

Rust (4) *Long loop:* Punch a single row to make the part in the hair. *Short loop:* Outline and fill in the areas on either side of the face between the hair and the shoulders. Fill in the two small triangles on the sides of the skirt at the bottom. Turn your burlap over. Working from the front, punch the outline of the face and the curvy line dividing the hands. Cut the yarn on the back.

Bright gold (1) *Long loop:* Outline the hair, and then fill in alternate rows, leaving the in-between rows bare. *Short loop:* Outline and fill in the two large inverted triangles at the top of the skirt, and the one smaller one in the center below.

Pale gold (2) *Long loop:* Fill in the alternate rows of hair. Outline and fill in the lower half of each sleeve. Outline and fill in the large triangles on either side of the skirt.

Check for any skimpy spots and fill in if necessary.

See Chapter 11 for instructions for trimming your pillow, and Chapter 12 for finishing it.

VARIATIONS

Because this pattern is so geometric, it's easy to substitute other colors. Try purple for the bodice and royal blue in place of the fuschia in the skirt and sleeves. Or make Mother a redhead by punching her hair in red or orange and replacing the rust with black. You don't have to stick to obvious colors, either. You can give her two-toned green or blue hair if you want to make her look somewhat unusual. If you do, though, be sure to liven up the look of your pillow by using bright contrasting colors in the top and bottom of the dress.

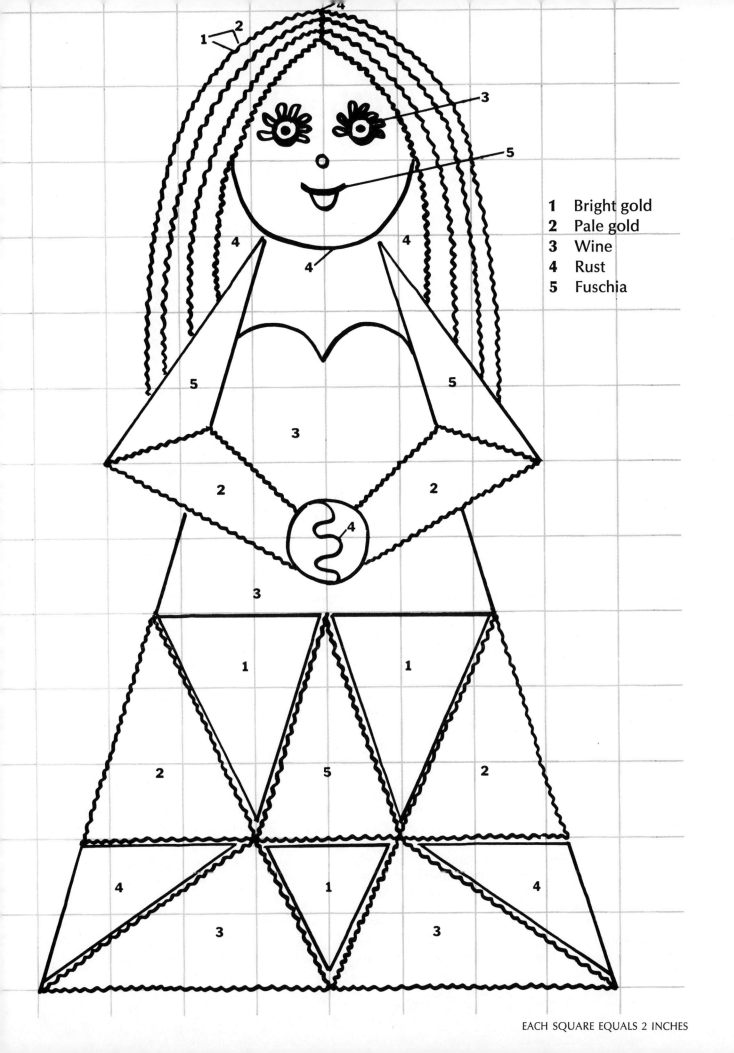

1 Bright gold
2 Pale gold
3 Wine
4 Rust
5 Fuschia

EACH SQUARE EQUALS 2 INCHES

Mother II

MATERIALS

Burlap: 30″ × 16″ (tape the edges)
Yarn: dark brown, 60 yards
    rust, 30 yards
    grass green, 40 yards
    red orange, 25 yards
    dark olive, 40 yards

TRIM

2 dark green eye buttons
1 small pink nose button

FOR FINISHING

Iron-on interfacing: 28″ × 14″
Backing: 30″ × 16″
Stuffing: 1¼ pounds polyester fiber

TRANSFERRING THE DESIGN

Leave a 2-inch margin on all sides and draw a grid of 2-inch squares, 13 squares high by 6 squares wide, with your blue felt marker.

Locate the nose and bustline as key points on your grid. Copy the rest of the design, square by square, from the illustration. Note that the chinline dips slightly into the fourth row down and that the bottom of the skirt dips deeply into the bottom squares. Check against the centerline to make sure the sides are equal. Go over the finished drawing with your black felt marker.

PUNCHING THE DESIGN

Dark brown (1) *Long loop:* Outline the hair entirely, then punch two rows within the hair area all around the head but haphazardly rather than in even rows. Punch the eyelashes. (The eye buttons will be added later as "trim.") *Short loop:* Fill in the upper half of the first band of the skirt. Skip one row, then fill in the lower half. Punch the curvy line that runs across the third band of the skirt, but don't make

the curve too steep—it should half fill the area only. Starting from the outside, punch the curvy line on each cuff. Starting from the outside and working in toward the center, punch three rows to make each circle in the fourth band of the skirt. (The center of the circles will be filled with rust later.)

Grass green (3) *Long loop:* Punch one row across to separate the fourth band from the fifth band of the skirt. *Short loop:* Outline and fill in the background of the second band of the skirt, leaving the circles bare for the moment. Outline the bodice and the upper sleeve area and fill in, but leave the bustline and the spaces between the arms and the body unpunched as these will be done in dark olive later.

Red orange (4) *Short loop:* Outline and fill in the background in the fourth band of the skirt. Working in toward the center, punch two rows for each circle in the collar, and three rows for each circle in the second band of the skirt. Turn your burlap over. Working from the front, outline the mouth. Cut the yarn on the back.

Rust (2) *Long loop:* Fill in the hair. Punch the one row that separates the upper and lower halves of the first band of the skirt. Make two or three punches in the center of each circle in the collar and in the second and fourth bands of the skirt. *Short loop:* Punch a second curvy line alongside the dark brown one, across the third band of the skirt. Punch a curvy line alongside the curvy line in each cuff to fill those areas.

Dark olive (5) *Long loop:* Punch one row across the top of the skirt to separate it from the bodice. Punch one row across to separate the first band of the skirt from the second. Punch two rows across to separate the second and third bands and to fill the area above the curvy line in the third band. Punch two rows across just below the curvy lines to separate the third band from the fourth band. Outline the fifth band of the skirt and fill it in. *Short loop:* Outline the collar and fill in the background. Punch one row to outline the bustline. Turn your burlap over. Working from the front, fill in the areas separating the arms from the body.

Check for any skimpy spots and fill in if necessary.

See Chapter 11 for instructions for trimming your pillow, and Chapter 12 for finishing it.

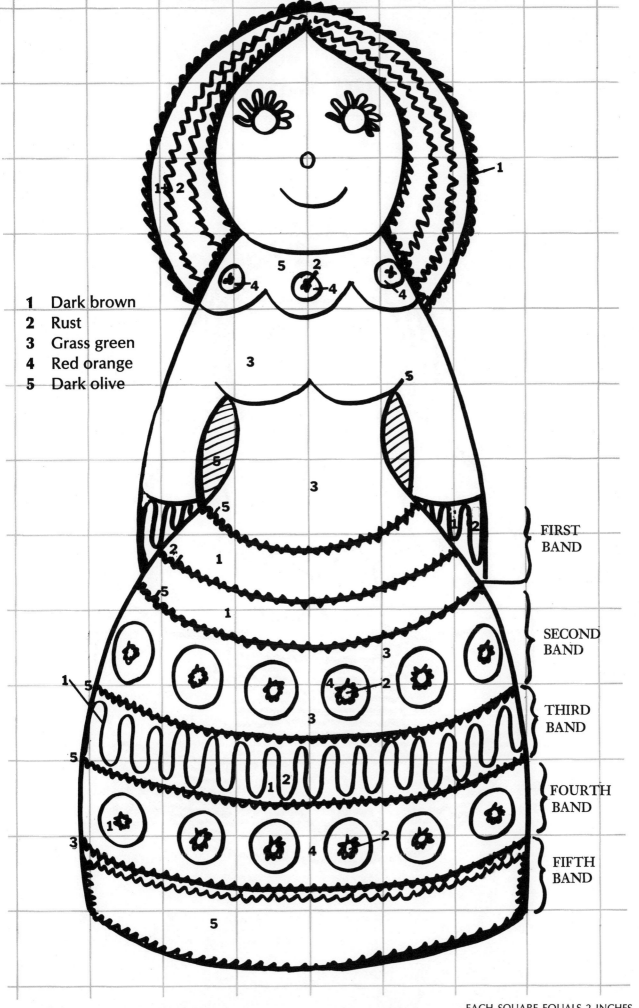

1 Dark brown
2 Rust
3 Grass green
4 Red orange
5 Dark olive

FIRST BAND

SECOND BAND

THIRD BAND

FOURTH BAND

FIFTH BAND

EACH SQUARE EQUALS 2 INCHES

The Baby

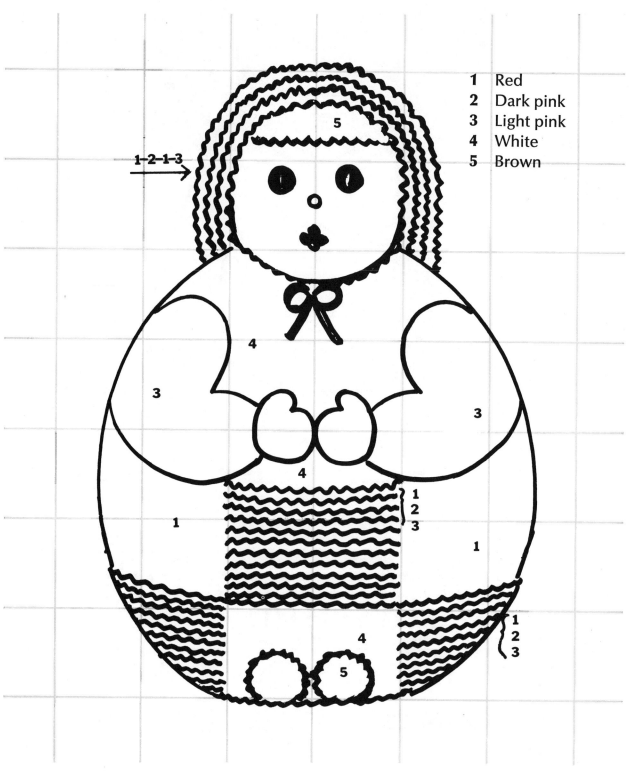

1 Red
2 Dark pink
3 Light pink
4 White
5 Brown

1-2-1-3

EACH SQUARE EQUALS 2 INCHES

MATERIALS

Burlap: 16″ × 18″ (tape the edges)
Yarn: red, 25 yards
      dark pink, 10 yards
      light pink, 20 yards
      white, 15 yards
      brown, 5 yards

TRIM

2 black eye buttons
1 pink nose button
1 pink yarn bow

FOR FINISHING

Iron-on interfacing: 14″ × 16″
Backing: 16″ × 18″
Stuffing: ½ pound polyester fiber

TRANSFERRING THE DESIGN

Leave a 2-inch margin on all sides and draw a grid of 2-inch squares, 7 squares high by 6 squares wide, with your blue felt marker.

Locate the nose, hands and feet as key points on your grid. Then copy the design, square by square, with your blue felt marker.

It's not necessary to draw all the wavy lines. Just outline the long-loop areas and remember to change color as explained below. Check against the centerline to make sure the sides are equal. Go over the finished drawing with your black felt marker.

PUNCHING THE DESIGN

Red (1) *Long loop:* Starting from the outside, punch one row around the outside of the head. Skip one row and punch another row around the head, leaving a row in between to be punched in dark pink (2) and the outline of the face in light pink (3) later. Next, punch the top row across the area marked with wavy lines in the center of the body. The sequence in this area, and in the two areas on the lower sides also marked with wavy lines, is red, dark pink, light pink, repeated four times. There's no need for you to cut your yarn when you reach the end of the first row. Just skip two rows and punch another row across in the opposite direction. Without cutting your yarn again, skip two rows and punch a third row; then skip two rows and punch a fourth row to complete the red in this area. Follow the same procedure in the two side areas. Then punch one row to outline the bottom of the body. *Short loop:* Outline and fill in the areas on each side beneath the arms.

Dark pink (2) *Long loop:* Punch one row around the head between the two rows of red. Then, following the same procedure as with the red, punch one row across the center area just beneath each row of red. Do not cut your yarn—just skip two rows and punch another across in the opposite direction until you have completed four rows. Follow the same procedure in the two side areas. *Short loop:* Turn your burlap over. Working from the front, make three punches for the mouth—one on top and two below. Cut the yarn on the back.

Light pink (3) *Long loop:* Punch one row completely around the face, outlining the chin and hairline. Then, following the same procedure as with the red and dark pink, punch one row across the center area of the body beneath each row of dark pink, skipping two rows each time and without cutting your yarn. Repeat the procedure in the two side areas in the lower part of the body. *Short loop:* Outline and fill in the two arms.

Brown (5) *Long loop:* Fill in the hair area just above the face. Outline and fill in the two feet.

White (4) *Short loop:* Outline and fill in the body above the arms up to the chin and the area below the hands, but leave the hands bare. Fill in the area at the bottom around the feet.

Check for any skimpy spots and fill in if necessary.

See Chapter 11 for instructions for trimming your pillow, and Chapter 12 for finishing it.

VARIATIONS

You may, of course, make the baby any colors you choose. If you want to make a traditional boy baby, use three shades of blue, and substitute yellow or gold for the white. If you're punching the pillow for an expectant mother, you can hedge your bet by using three shades of green or yellow, and a contrasting color in place of the white. When you're combining shades this way, it's helpful to hold your yarns together in the store before you buy them, to make sure the colors harmonize with each other.

Little Brother

MATERIALS

Burlap: red, 16″ × 24″ (tape the edges)
Yarn: black, 20 yards
    royal blue, 40 yards
    maroon, 30 yards
    gray, 20 yards
    hot pink, 40 yards

TRIM

2 purple eye buttons
1 pink nose button
1 pink belly button
2 gray yarn shoe bows

FOR FINISHING

Iron-on interfacing: 14″ × 22″
Backing: 16″ × 24″
Stuffing: 1½ pounds polyester fiber

TRANSFERRING THE DESIGN

Leave a 2-inch margin on all sides and draw a grid of 2-inch squares, 10 squares high by 6 squares wide, with your blue felt marker.

Locate the nose, chin, belly button and the line dividing the legs as key points on your grid. Copy the rest of the design, square by square, from the illustration. Check against the centerline to make sure the sides are equal. Then go over the finished drawing with your black felt marker.

PUNCHING THE DESIGN

Black (1) *Long loop:* Outline the hair, then fill it in. *Short loop:* Outline the belt and fill in, but leave the belt buckle bare. Punch one row for the line dividing the legs. Punch one row for the line separating the arms from the body.

Royal blue (2) *Long loop:* Punch two rows

across the top of the pants, just above the belt. Then outline and fill in the short pants below the belt. *Short loop:* Outline and fill in the right, left, and center sections of the beanie. Outline and fill in the main part of the sneakers, leaving the tips and inner circles bare for the moment.

Maroon (3) *Long loop:* Add some color to the hair by punching a few random loops in the hair area. *Short loop:* Outline and fill in the yoke of the T-shirt at the top. Then punch four rows to outline and fill the two separate stripes of maroon in the center and lower areas of the T-shirt. Change the direction of the stripes when you reach the arms, as shown in the illustration. Outline and fill in the alternate stripes in the socks. Then turn your burlap over. Working from the front, punch one row for the line of the mouth. Cut the yarn on the back. Working from the front again, punch the outside line of the legs between the bottom of the shorts and the top of the socks.

Gray (4) *Long loop:* Punch two rows for the soles of the sneakers. *Short loop:* Fill in the toes and circles of the sneakers. Punch one row across the top of each sneaker, and one row between them to separate them. Fill in the belt buckle. Punch two rows across to make each of the four gray stripes of the T-shirt, changing direction across the arms as shown in the illustration. Fill in the two remaining sections of the beanie.

Hot pink (5) *Short loop:* Punch 6 rows across for the center stripe in the T-shirt, changing direction when you reach the arms. Fill in the upper hot pink stripe in the T-shirt between the gray stripe and the yoke. Outline the outer edge of the socks and fill in the alternate stripes as indicated.

Check for any skimpy spots and fill in if necessary.

See Chapter 11 for instructions for trimming your pillow, and Chapter 12 for finishing it.

VARIATIONS

You don't have to use red burlap for Little Brother's skin color—you can use brown, yellow, pink or natural, if you prefer. You can also change

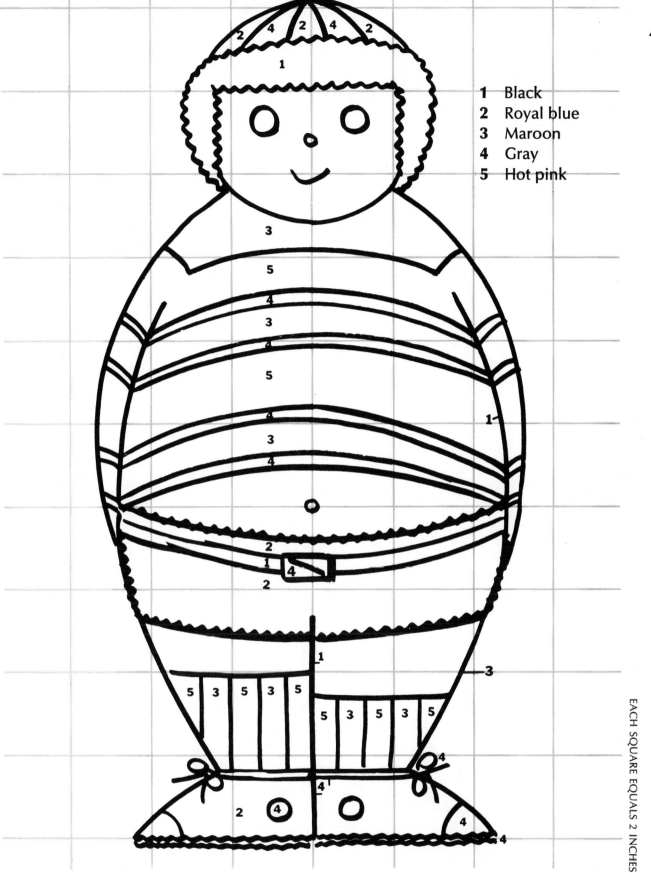

1 Black
2 Royal blue
3 Maroon
4 Gray
5 Hot pink

49

EACH SQUARE EQUALS 2 INCHES

the colors of the stripes on his T-shirt, or make the shirt a solid color and have him wearing vertically striped shorts. If you do change the colors, repeat the beanie colors in the sneakers and the T-shirt colors in the socks so that you maintain a color balance in your over-all design.

Little Sister

MATERIALS

Burlap: 24″ × 12″ (tape the edges)
Yarn: brown, 15 yards
    rust, 15 yards
    rose, 25 yards
    cream, 25 yards
    plum, 18 yards
    pale gold, 8 yards
    olive, 25 yards

TRIM

1 pink nose button
2 purple eye buttons
1 pale gold yarn hair bow

FOR FINISHING

Iron-on interfacing: 22″ × 10″
Backing: 24″ × 12″
Stuffing: ¾ pound polyester fiber

TRANSFERRING THE DESIGN

Leave a 2-inch margin on all sides and draw a grid of 2-inch squares, 10 squares high by 4 squares wide, with your blue felt marker.

Locate the line of the bangs, the line of the collar and the line of the hem as key points on your grid. Then copy the rest of the design, square by square, from the illustration. Check against the centerline to make sure the sides are equal. Go over the finished drawing with your black felt marker.

PUNCHING THE DESIGN

Brown (1) *Long loop:* Outline the hair, from shoulder to shoulder, around the outside of the head and the face. Punch two more rows along each side of the face. Punch five rows from the top of the head down to the edge of the bangs.

Rust (2) *Long loop:* Fill in the remaining hair area. *Short loop:* Punch the dividing line between the socks, but leave the upper part of the leg bare for the moment. Then turn your burlap over. Working from the front, outline the chin, the arms below the sleeves and the hands and fingers. Still working from the front, outline the legs above the socks and the mouth. Cut the yarn on the back.

Rose (3) *Short loop:* Outline and fill in the top part of the collar up to the chin. Punch one row across the center of each sleeve cuff, and two rows across the skirt of the dress above the border. Outline and fill in the socks, leaving bare two rows for the horizontal stripes.

Plum (5) *Long loop:* Punch the zigzag line across the collar and across the bottom of the skirt. Outline the shoes and fill them in. Punch one line for the shoestrap across each ankle.

Cream (4) *Short loop:* Fill in the sleeve cuffs. Punch one row across each sock. Then fill in the background of the collar and the bottom area of the skirt, around the zigzag stripes.

Pale gold (6) *Long loop:* Punch one row across the bottom of the collar. Punch one row across the bottom of the skirt, and one row straight across the top of the zigzag line on the skirt. Punch one row at the bottom of each sleeve cuff where it joins the arm.

Olive (7) *Short loop:* Outline and fill in the dress area above and below the arms down to the rose stripe. Punch three rows across the skirt below the rose stripe. Punch one row across each sock, below the cream stripe.

Check for any skimpy spots and fill in if necessary.

See Chapter 11 for instructions for trimming your pillow, and Chapter 12 for finishing it.

1 Brown
2 Rust
3 Rose
4 Cream
5 Plum
6 Pale gold
7 Olive

EACH SQUARE EQUALS 2 INCHES

Little Black Sister

MATERIALS

Burlap: brown, 26″ × 16″ (tape the edges)
Yarn: black, 30 yards
 hot pink, 28 yards
 red, 25 yards
 light pink, 25 yards
 royal blue, 10 yards
 white, 35 yards

TRIM

2 eye buttons (preferably with some white to show up against the brown burlap)
1 brown nose button
2 white pearl shoe buttons
1 hot pink yarn hair bow

FOR FINISHING

Iron-on interfacing: 24″ × 14″
Backing: 26″ × 16″
Stuffing: 1 pound polyester fiber

TRANSFERRING THE DESIGN

Leave a 2-inch margin on all sides and draw a grid of 2-inch squares, 11 squares high by 6 squares wide, with your blue felt marker.

Locate the nose, hands and hemline as key points on your grid. Copy the rest of the design, square by square, from the illustration. Check against the centerline to make sure the sides are equal. Go over the finished drawing with your black felt marker.

PUNCHING THE DESIGN

Black (1) *Long loop:* Outline the hair and fill in. Outline the toes of the shoes and fill in. *Short loop:*
Turn your burlap over. Working from the front, outline the hands and fingers. Then punch one row to separate the bare legs above the socks. Cut the yarn on the back.

Red (3) *Long loop:* Outline and fill in the outside stripes on the dress, above and below the sleeves. *Short loop:* Outline and fill in the socks, above the spats.

Hot pink (2) *Long loop:* Outline and fill in the second stripe on either side of the dress, above and below the arms. *Short loop:* Turn your burlap over. Working from the front, punch the mouth. Cut the yarn on the back.

Light pink (4) *Long loop:* Outline and fill in the center panel of the dress above and below the hands. *Short loop:* Fill in the sleeves.

Royal blue (5) *Long loop:* Punch one row along the entire edge of the collar, and one row along the edge of each sleeve where it joins the arm. Punch one row along the bottom of the dress. *Short loop:* Punch one row to separate the legs from the shoes up to the top of the socks.

White (6) *Short loop:* Fill in the collar and the two remaining stripes on the dress. Fill in the spats between the shoe tips and the socks.

Check for any skimpy spots and fill in if necessary.

See Chapter 11 for instructions for trimming your pillow, and Chapter 12 for finishing it.

VARIATIONS

You can, of course, make this design on any color burlap you like or change the colors of the dress, or both. Alternate stripes of dark blue, medium blue and light blue combined with yellow instead of white make an attractive dress. So do three different shades of green combined with gold. Be sure to repeat the color of the collar in the spats for color balance, and to use a contrasting color to edge the collar, sleeves and hemline.

1 Black
2 Hot pink
3 Red
4 Light pink
5 Royal blue
6 White

EACH SQUARE EQUALS 2 INCHES

Big Brother

MATERIALS

Burlap: 30″ × 16″ (tape the edges)
Yarn: yellow orange, 15 yards
　　　lemon yellow, 10 yards
　　　royal blue, 65 yards
　　　white, 30 yards
　　　red, 45 yards

TRIM

2 blue eye buttons
1 pink nose button
2 brass curtain rings for eyeglasses

FOR FINISHING

Iron-on interfacing: 28″ × 14″
Backing: 30″ × 16″
Stuffing: 1¼ pounds polyester fiber

TRANSFERRING THE DESIGN

Leave a 2-inch margin on all sides and draw a grid of 2-inch squares, 13 squares high and 6 squares wide, with your blue felt marker.

Locate the nose, the bottom of the sweater and the points of the shoes as key points on your grid. Copy the rest of the design, square by square, from the illustration. Haphazard lines in the hair indicate haphazard punches for color and texture—there's no need to copy them exactly. Check against the centerline to make sure the sides are equal. Go over the final drawing with your black felt marker.

PUNCHING THE DESIGN

Red (5) *Long loop:* Outline the pants and fill in. *Short loop:* Outline the inside of the arms. Turn your burlap over. Working from the front, punch the line of the mouth. Cut the yarn on the back.

Royal blue (3) *Long loop:* Punch one row to separate the legs. *Short loop:* Punch two rows to separate the shoes, two rows across the bottom for the shoe soles and two rows for each of the stripes on the shoes. Then outline the sweater from the top of the border at the bottom up to the collar, including the sleeves, omitting only the outside edges of the sleeve stripes. Outline the outside border of the letter Y. Then fill in the entire sweater except for the Y and three rows for each of the stripes on the sleeves.

Yellow orange (1) *Long loop:* Outline the hair, then punch a few haphazard rows in the hair area. *Short loop:* Punch two rows around the Y to make the border. Outline and fill in the circles on the shoes. Turn your burlap over. Working from the front, punch one row along the outer edge of each hand. Cut the yarn on the back.

Lemon yellow (2) *Long loop:* Fill in the hair area. *Short loop:* Fill in the Y on the sweater.

White (4) *Short loop:* Outline the collar and fill in. Punch three rows for each sleeve stripe. Outline and fill in the border at the bottom of the sweater. Fill in the remaining bare areas of the shoes.

Check for any skimpy spots and fill in if necessary.

See Chapter 11 for instructions for trimming your pillow, and Chapter 12 for finishing it.

VARIATIONS

You can change Big Brother's uniform to correspond to any school colors you fancy. If you do change any colors, repeat the hair or sweater color in the shoes. If you change the letter on his sweater, remember you're working from the back, so when you're transferring the design to your burlap, be sure to make the letter (or number) in reverse unless it's an A, H, I, M, O, T, U, V, W, X or Y.

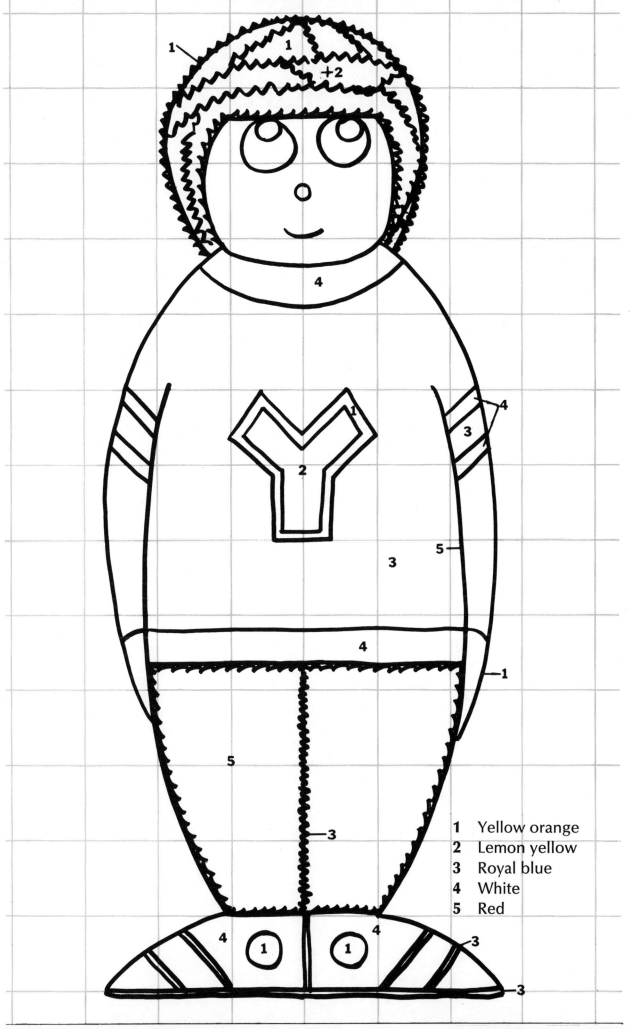

55

1 Yellow orange
2 Lemon yellow
3 Royal blue
4 White
5 Red

EACH SQUARE EQUALS 2 INCHES

56

Big Sister

MATERIALS

Burlap: 30″ × 16″ (tape the edges)
Yarn: gold, 50 yards
    rust, 10 yards
    red, 40 yards
    light gray, 25 yards
    sky blue, 25 yards
    turquoise, 25 yards
    navy blue, 10 yards

TRIM

2 blue eye buttons
1 pink nose button
2 red or blue plastic or brass curtain rings for earrings

FOR FINISHING

Iron-on interfacing: 28″ × 14″
Backing: 30″ × 16″
Stuffing: 1¼ pounds polyester fiber

TRANSFERRING THE DESIGN

Leave a 2-inch margin on all sides and draw a grid of 2-inch squares, 13 squares high by 6 squares wide, with your blue felt marker.

Locate the top of the head, the waistline and the line dividing the legs as key points. The dotted circles indicate where the earrings are attached—you don't have to include them on your drawing. Copy the rest of the design, square by square, from the illustration. Check against the centerline to make sure the sides are equal. Go over the finished drawing with your black felt marker.

PUNCHING THE DESIGN

Navy blue (7) *Short loop:* Outline the shoulder straps. Punch two thick vertical stripes from the top of the bodice of the overalls to the waistline. Then punch one row across the top of the overalls and one across the waistline. Outline one pocket from the bottom of the hand to the thumb, then continue across the V-shaped line defining the top of the thighs to outline the pocket on the other side. Punch the line separating the legs of the overalls to the cuffs, and outline the cuffs.

Red (3) *Short loop:* Outline the shirt sleeves and fill in. Outline the center area of the shirt between the shoulder straps and above the overalls and fill in. Leave the straps bare for the moment. Turn your burlap over. Working from the front, punch the mouth line. Cut the yarn on the back.

Turquoise (6) *Short loop:* Following the centerline of the overalls, punch one row running down from the top to the line dividing the legs. Punch one vertical row in the center of each shoulder strap. Note: The sequence of the vertical stripes in the overalls from the centerline out to each side is turquoise, light gray, sky blue, until you reach the edge. This sequence is repeated in the shoulder straps. After you have punched one row of light gray and one row of sky blue on either side of the turquoise, repeat the turquoise and continue the sequence in both areas.

Light gray (4) *Short loop:* Punch one row on either side of the turquoise (and navy blue) centerline from the top of the overalls down to the trouser cuffs. Fill in the cuffs, leaving room for one row of sky blue across the center. See the Note under Turquoise for the continuation of the stripes in the overalls.

Sky blue (5) *Short loop:* Punch one row on either side of the light gray from the top of the

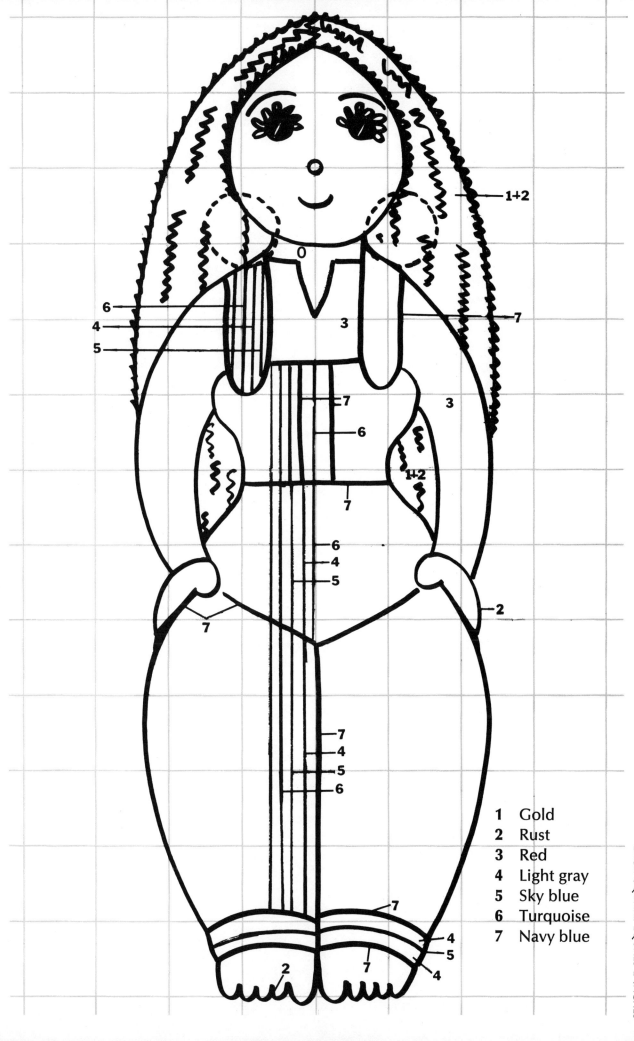

1+2

6
4
5

3

7

0

3

7

6

1+2

7

6
4
5

2

7

7
4
5
6

7

7
4
5
4

2

1 Gold
2 Rust
3 Red
4 Light gray
5 Sky blue
6 Turquoise
7 Navy blue

EACH SQUARE EQUALS 2 INCHES

58

overalls to the cuffs. Punch one row across the center of each cuff. See the Note under Turquoise for the continuation of the stripes in the overalls.

Gold (1) *Long loop:* Outline the hair completely and fill in, but loosely, so that you'll be able to add some haphazard punches of rust. *Short loop:* Turn your burlap over. Working from the front, fill in the areas between the body and the arms, but loosely again, so that you'll be able to add some haphazard rust punches. Cut the yarn on the back.

Rust (2) *Long loop:* Complete the hair with haphazard punches. *Short loop:* Add some haphazard punches to the area between the body and the arms. Then turn your burlap over and, working from the front, outline the chin and the eyebrows. Still working from the front, outline the hands, toes and the line dividing the feet. Cut the yarn on the back.

Check for any skimpy spots and fill in if necessary.

See Chapter 11 for instructions for trimming your pillow, and Chapter 12 for finishing it.

VARIATIONS

You can easily change the hair color to any shade you prefer, but the hair will look more interesting if you use two colors—dark brown with haphazard punches of rust, for example, or black with blue.

The shirt in the photograph was made by using two strands of worsted together—one bright red and one plum—rather than the red rug-and-craft yarn the instructions call for. If you prefer this tweedy look, you'll need 40 yards of each color worsted. Take two balls of equal length and thread a strand from each through the punch needle so that you can punch them together (see page 18).

You can simplify Big Sister by making her overalls one solid color and punching the heavy black lines on the design with a contrasting color. Or you can make her overalls a solid color and put stripes on her shirt. Don't be afraid to experiment—you can always pull out your loops and punch in something else.

Girl Rider

MATERIALS

Burlap: 30″ × 16″ (tape the edges)
Yarn: blue, 70 yards
      brown, 15 yards
      black, 15 yards
      coral, 10 yards
      cream, 30 yards
      wine, 40 yards

TRIM

2 brown eye buttons
1 pink nose button
3 round brass buttons for the jacket
2 brass curtain rings for earrings
1 medal or prize ribbon

FOR FINISHING

Iron-on interfacing: 28″ × 14″
Backing: 30″ × 16″
Stuffing: 1 pound polyester fiber

TRANSFERRING THE DESIGN

Leave a 2-inch margin on all sides and draw a grid of 2-inch squares, 13 squares high by 6 squares wide, with your blue felt marker.

Locate the nose, the bottom of the jacket and the top of the boots as key points on your grid.

Copy the rest of the design, square by square, from the illustration. The dotted lines indicate where the earrings and the medal are attached—you don't have to include them on your drawing. Check against the centerline to make sure the sides are

1	Blue	**4**	Coral
2	Brown	**5**	Cream
3	Black	**6**	Wine

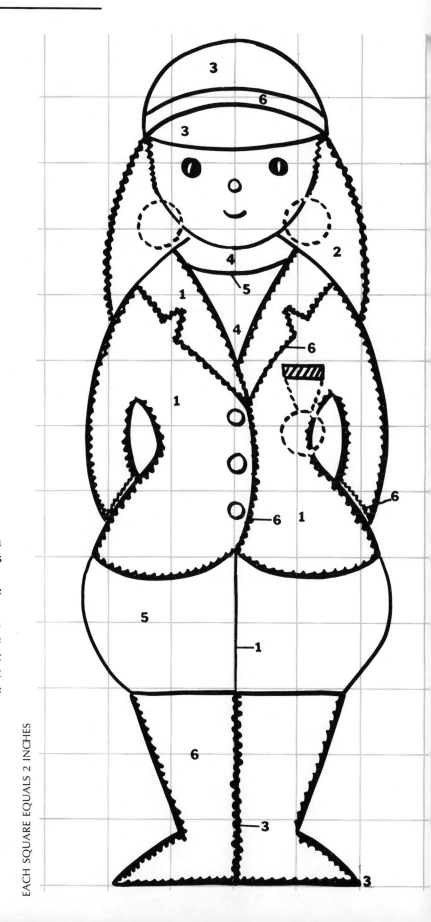

EACH SQUARE EQUALS 2 INCHES

equal. Go over the finished drawing with your black felt marker.

PUNCHING THE DESIGN

Wine (6) *Long loop:* Punch one row to outline the edge of the lapels. Continue down the edge of the jacket until you reach the line dividing the legs. Then outline the bottom edge of both sleeves. Outline and fill in the boots, but for the moment leave bare the vertical row dividing the boots and the soles of the boots. *Short loop:* Outline and fill in the ribbon across the hat. Turn your burlap over and, working from the front, punch the mouth. Cut the yarn on the back.

Blue (1) *Long loop:* Outline and fill in the jacket including the sleeves. Leave the space between the arms and waist unpunched. *Short loop:* Punch the dividing line in the center of the breeches.

Brown (2) *Long loop:* Outline the hair on both sides of the face and fill in.

Black (3) *Long loop:* Punch the dividing line between the boots. Punch two rows across the bottom of the feet for the soles. *Short loop:* Outline the top part of the hat and fill it in, then outline and fill in the visor.

Coral (4) *Short loop:* Fill in the shirt area, but skip one row for the stripe near the neck.

Cream (5) *Short loop:* Punch the stripe across the top of the shirt. Outline and fill in the breeches.

Check for any skimpy spots and fill in if necessary.

See Chapter 11 for instructions for trimming your pillow, and Chapter 12 for finishing it. See photographs on page 12.

VARIATIONS

You can vary the colors of the rider's habit to suit yourself. Punch the boots black if you wish, and the jacket a lighter shade of blue. But whatever changes you make, keep the dividing line between the boots the same color as the ribbon on the hat.

Father

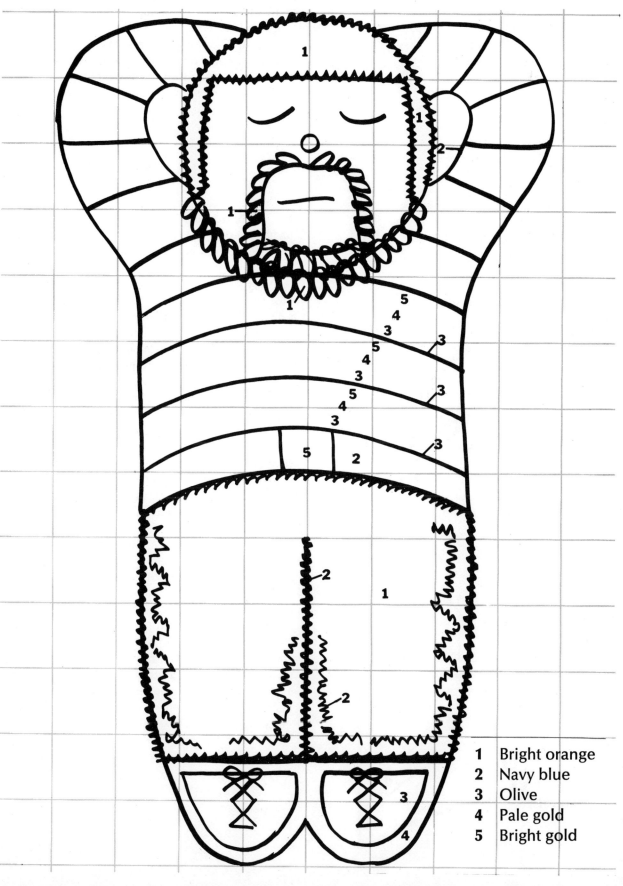

1 Bright orange
2 Navy blue
3 Olive
4 Pale gold
5 Bright gold

EACH SQUARE EQUALS 2 INCHES

MATERIALS

Burlap: gold, 30″ × 20″ (tape the edges)
Yarn: bright orange, 100 yards
    navy blue, 20 yards
    olive, 30 yards
    pale gold, 30 yards
    bright gold, 25 yards

TRIM

1 nose button
2 bright gold yarn shoelaces

FOR FINISHING

Iron-on interfacing: 28″ × 18″
Backing: 30″ × 20″
Stuffing: 1½ pounds polyester fiber

EACH SQUARE EQUALS 2 INCHES

TRANSFERRING THE DESIGN

Leave a 2-inch margin on all sides and draw a grid of 2-inch squares, 13 squares high by 8 squares wide, with your blue felt marker.

Locate the nose, ears and belt as key points on your grid. Then copy the rest of the design, square by square, from the illustration. Check against the centerline to make sure the sides are equal. Go over the finished drawing with your black felt marker.

PUNCHING THE DESIGN

Bright orange (1) *Long loop:* Outline the hair and sideburns, and fill in. Outline and fill in the pants, but skip the line dividing the legs. *Extra long loop:* Punch the beard and moustache (see page 28 for instructions).

Navy blue (2) *Long loop:* Punch one row to divide the pants legs. Punch haphazard loops on either side of the dividing line to add color and texture to the pants. *Short loop:* Punch five rows across to make the belt, but leave the buckle bare for the moment. Outline the ears, and punch one row for each closed eye. Turn your burlap over and, working from the front, punch the line of the mouth. Cut the yarn on the back.

Olive (3) *Short loop:* Each line on the design going across the shirt and on up the sleeves represents the beginning of a sequence—olive, pale gold, bright gold—from bottom to top. Starting just above the belt, punch four rows across the shirt. Fill in the inside of the shoes, leaving the borders bare for the moment.

Pale gold (4) *Short loop:* Punch three rows across the shirt, just above the olive. Outline and fill in the border of the shoes.

Bright gold (5) *Short loop:* Outline and fill in the belt buckle. Punch two rows across the shirt just above the pale gold. Note: You can now continue the sequence of four rows of olive, three of pale gold and two of bright gold up the rest of the shirt and on up each sleeve. The stripes become wedge-shaped as you approach the elbow and the actual number of punches will vary—more will be required on the outer side of the arm. Just be sure you start with olive each time you hit a line. For the last section, where the arms disappear behind the head, use olive only.

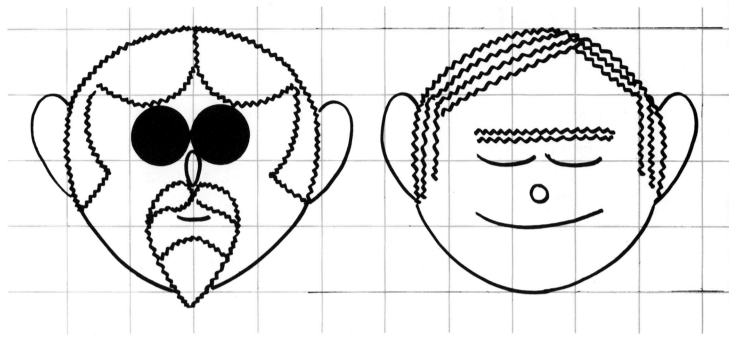

EACH SQUARE EQUALS 2 INCHES

Check for any skimpy spots and fill in if necessary.

See Chapter 11 for instructions for trimming your pillow, and Chapter 12 for finishing it.

VARIATIONS

It is a simple matter to change any part of Father except the fact that he's lying down taking a nap. You can change his color scheme, the style of his shoes, give him a different kind of shirt or put stripes in his pants. Here are three suggestions to use as is, or to start you thinking of your own variations.

1. You can make him a snoozing dandy with a handlebar moustache and a vest. Punch in the hair, eyebrows, moustache and cravat with long loop. Use short loop for the collar, sleeves and vest. Outline the pockets on the vest with short loop in a contrasting color. Give him a diamond button for a stickpin.

2. You can make him elegant with a Van Dyke beard and dark glasses. Use big brown or black buttons for the dark glasses. Use long loop gray and black for his hair and beard, and put stripes in his pants by alternating rows of gray and black.

3. Perhaps Father is just an all-American boy with nice, bushy eyebrows and a smile on his face because he is having pleasant dreams.

(NOTE: The Father pillow in the color photograph is slightly different from the design in that his beard begins before the pale gold and bright gold complete the stripe sequence under the chin.)

Dapper Uncle Dudley

MATERIALS

Burlap: pink, 30″ × 16″ (tape the edges)
Yarn: black, 50 yards
  blue, 50 yards
  white, 20 yards
  red, 20 yards
  pink, 15 yards
  maroon, 15 yards

TRIM

2 blue eye buttons
1 round red nose button
6 round brass vest buttons
1 diamond button for a tiepin
7-inch gold watch chain

FOR FINISHING

Iron-on interfacing: 28″ × 14″
Backing: 30″ × 16″
Stuffing: 1¼ pounds polyester fiber

TRANSFERRING THE DESIGN

Leave a 2-inch margin on all sides and draw a grid of 2-inch squares, 13 squares high by 6 squares wide, with your blue felt marker.

Locate the eyebrows, chinline, the V-shape of the top of the vest and the shoe tips as key points on your grid. Note that the shoes rest on the bottom line of the grid but that the head doesn't quite reach the top. There's no need to draw the stripes in the pants. Copy the rest of the design, square by square, from the illustration. Check against the centerline to make sure the sides are equal. Go over your final drawing with your black felt marker.

PUNCHING THE DESIGN

Black (1) *Long loop:* Starting from the tip of the handlebar moustache, punch two rows around the head for the hair. Then outline and fill in the moustache. Punch two rows across for the eyebrows. Punch the line separating the sleeves from the jacket and the outside edge of the lapels. Punch two rows down the centerline of the pants. Then, working away from the centerline, punch alternate vertical rows to make the black stripes of the pants. You won't have to cut your yarn until you reach the outside edge of one leg—just punch down one row, skip one row and come up the next. *Short loop:* Outline and fill in the toe and heel areas on each shoe. Punch the line separating the shoes.

Blue (2) *Long loop:* Outline the jacket and fill in. Now punch alternate vertical stripes between the black stripes on the pants in the same manner described above.

Red (4) *Long loop:* Outline the tie and fill in. *Short loop:* Punch one row for each vertical and horizontal line of the vest.

Pink (5) *Short loop:* Punch one row underneath each horizontal red line in the vest, and one row to the right of each vertical red line.

Maroon (6) *Short loop:* Punch one row above each horizontal red line in the vest and one to the left of each vertical red line. Turn your burlap over and, working from the front, outline the hands. Cut the yarn on the back.

White (3) *Short loop:* Outline and fill the rest of the shoe area. Fill in the collar, and add two rows at the end of each sleeve to make cuffs.

Check for any skimpy spots and fill in if necessary.

See Chapter 11 for instructions for trimming your pillow, and Chapter 12 for finishing it.

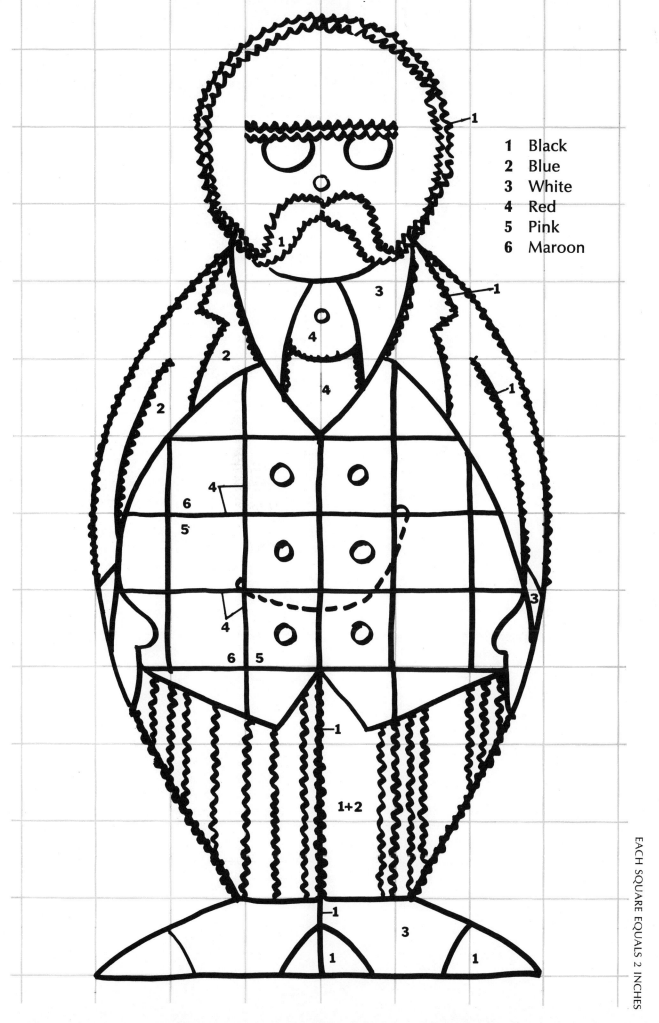

1 Black
2 Blue
3 White
4 Red
5 Pink
6 Maroon

EACH SQUARE EQUALS 2 INCHES

The Belly Dancer

MATERIALS

Burlap: 16″ × 30″ (tape the edges)
Yarn: black, 60 yards
purple, 40 yards
pale gold, 35 yards
wine, 40 yards
rust, 35 yards
lavender, 2 yards
hot pink, 2 yards

TRIM

2 black eye buttons
1 pink nose button
1 pink belly button
3 round gold buttons (1 for the center of the bra,
1 for each hip)

FOR FINISHING

Iron-on interfacing: 14″ × 28″
Backing: 16″ × 30″
Stuffing: 1¼ pounds polyester fiber

TRANSFERRING THE DESIGN

Leave a 2-inch margin on all sides and draw a grid of 2-inch squares, 13 squares high by 6 squares wide, with your blue felt marker.

Locate the headband, nose, chinline, centers of the breasts and centers of the hip ovals as key points on your grid. Note that the hips bulge slightly outside of the grid. Copy the rest of the design, square by square, from the illustration. Check against the centerline to make sure the sides are equal. Go over the finished drawing with your black felt marker.

PUNCHING THE DESIGN

Black (1) *Long loop:* Outline and fill in the hair on either side of the face and over the shoulders. Outline and fill the area at the bottom center. *Short loop:* Outline and fill in the gloved hand and the two arms up to the armbands. Leave the shoulders bare.

Purple (2) *Short loop:* Outline and fill in the crown of the hat. Then punch the zigzag line across the headband. Punch two rows around the outside of each breast. Punch three rows around the outside of each hip oval, and the stripe that runs across and connects them. Punch the zigzag lines across the center and the bottom stripes. Turn your burlap over. Working from the front, outline the eyelids. Cut the yarn on the back.

Wine (4) *Long loop:* Punch one row across the bottom of the headband. Punch two rows around the breasts, just inside the purple rows. Punch two rows just inside the purple rows on the hip ovals. Punch three rows across for the stripe below the purple stripe and above the zigzag at the bottom. *Short loop:* Outline and fill in the area at the top of the hips and around the hand. Turn your burlap over. Working from the front, punch the line dividing the lips. Cut the yarn on the back.

Rust (5) *Long loop:* Punch one row across the top of the headband. Punch three rows around the breasts, just inside the wine rows. Punch three rows around just inside the wine rows in the hip ovals. Then punch four rows across to make the stripes just above and below the center zigzag line.

Pale gold (3) *Long loop:* Fill the center of each breast, then fill the center of each hip oval. *Short loop:* Outline and fill in the collar. Outline and fill in the two arm bands. Fill in the background around the zigzag line of the headband and around the two zigzag lines in the bands of the skirt.

Lavender (6) *Short loop:* Working from the front, fill in the eyelids. Cut the yarn on the back.

Hot pink (7) *Short loop:* Working from the front, outline and fill in the upper and lower lips. Cut the yarn on the back.

Check for any skimpy spots and fill in if necessary.

See Chapter 11 for instructions for trimming your pillow, and Chapter 12 for finishing it.

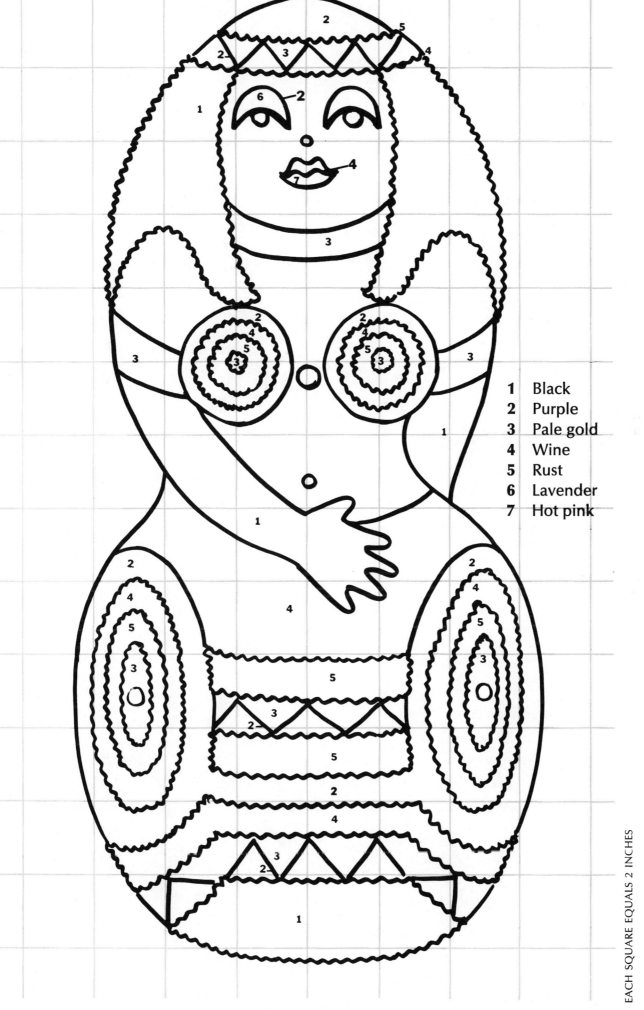

1 Black
2 Purple
3 Pale gold
4 Wine
5 Rust
6 Lavender
7 Hot pink

EACH SQUARE EQUALS 2 INCHES

CHAPTER
6
ANIMALS AND BIRDS

Here are some pets for your pillow people—though you may prefer to punch one of the animals or birds in this chapter first and then punch a person later.

The first four animals—the mouse, the cat and the two dogs—are very easy to transfer onto your burlap and to make. They're chiefly done in long loop, which not only comes out looking like fur but has the added advantage of concealing any mistakes you make in its shaggy tufts. The birds are mostly done in short loop, which captures the look of feathers more accurately but doesn't hide irregularities in the punching nearly as well.

You'll just have to be a little more careful when you're doing them unless you don't mind ending up with a slightly disheveled-looking owl or parrot.

As with all the designs in the book, you can, of course, vary any of these to suit your taste, or create your own totally different animals or birds. One caution, though—thin legs, particularly bird legs, can be a real problem if you're designing a shaped pillow. So try sitting your birds on a nest, or draw them in a square or rectangular setting and fill in the background with a simple, leafy pattern.

The Mouse

MATERIALS

Burlap: 10″ × 14″ (tape the edges)
Yarn: brown, 10 yards
    beige, 18 yards
    cream, 18 yards
    pink, 4 yards

TRIM

2 small round red eye buttons
pink and beige yarn tail

1	Brown	**3**	Cream
2	Beige	**4**	Pink

FOR FINISHING

Iron-on interfacing: 8″ × 12″
Backing: 10″ × 14″
Stuffing: ¼ pound polyester fiber

TRANSFERRING THE DESIGN

The mouse is simply a teardrop shape with two ears, two eyes, a nose and a tail. You can draw it freehand if you like, or if you lack confidence in your drawing ability, copy it onto a grid. In either case, there's no need to draw the tail—it's not punched, it's made separately and attached to the finished pillow as part of the trim.

Leave a 2-inch margin on all sides and draw a grid of 2-inch squares, 3 squares high by 5 squares wide, with your blue felt marker. Locate the nose in the lower lefthand corner of your grid as a key

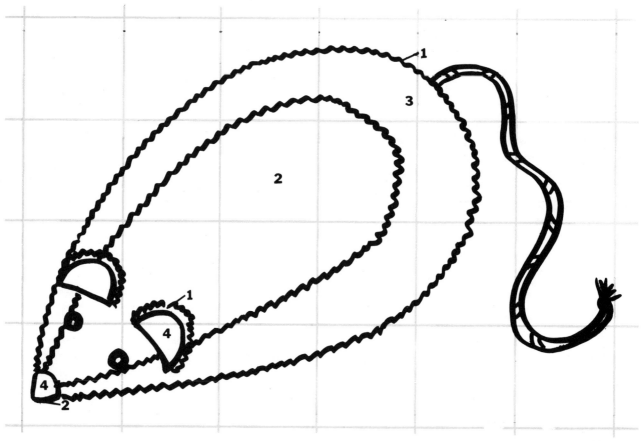

EACH SQUARE EQUALS 2 INCHES

point. Then, omitting the tail, copy the rest of the design, square by square, from the illustration. Go over the final drawing with your black felt marker.

PUNCHING THE DESIGN

Brown (1) *Long loop:* Outline the outside of the body. Outline the ears.

Beige (2) *Long loop:* Outline the center of the body and fill in. Outline the nose.

Cream (3) *Long loop:* Fill in the outer area of the body.

Pink (4) *Short loop:* Fill in the ears and the nose.

Check for any skimpy spots and fill in if necessary.

See Chapter 11 for instructions for trimming your pillow, and Chapter 12 for finishing it.

The Cat

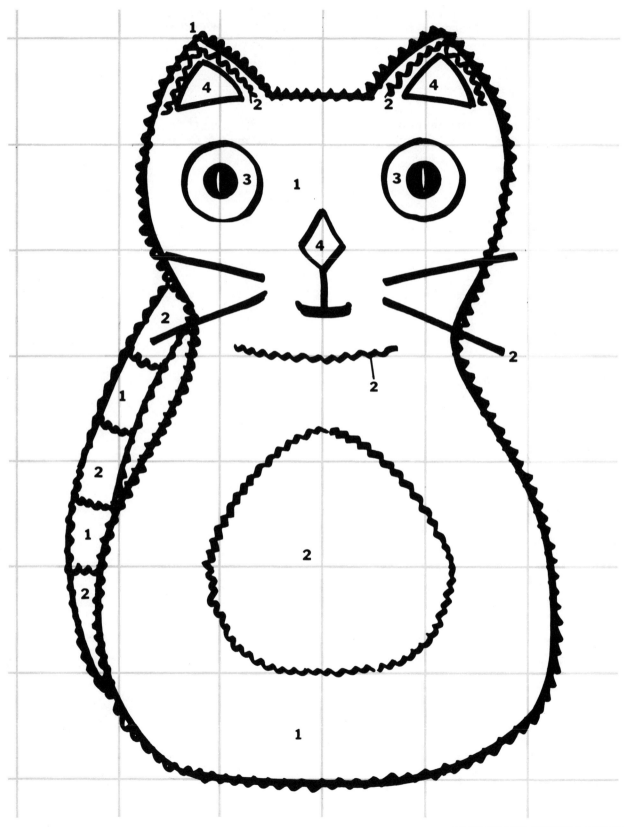

EACH SQUARE EQUALS 2 INCHES

MATERIALS

Burlap: 16″ × 18″ (tape the edges)
Yarn: maroon, 55 yards
    lavender, 25 yards
    turquoise, 3 yards
    coral, 5 yards

TRIM

2 purple eye buttons
lavender yarn whiskers

FOR FINISHING

Iron-on interfacing: 14″ × 16″
Backing: 16″ × 18″
Stuffing: ½ pound polyester fiber

TRANSFERRING THE DESIGN

Leave a 2-inch margin on all sides and draw a grid of 2-inch squares, 7 squares high by 6 squares wide, with your blue felt marker.

Locate the ears, nose and the two widest points of the body as key points on your grid. Copy the rest of the design, square by square, from the illustration. There's no need to draw the whiskers—they'll be added later as part of the trim. Check against the centerline to make sure the sides of the body are equal. (Note that the tail extends outside the body on the left side.) Go over the final drawing with your black felt marker.

PUNCHING THE DESIGN

Lavender (2) *Long loop:* Outline the circle in the center of the body, then fill it in by punching in a continuing spiral toward the center. Punch the chin line. Punch the inverted V above each ear. Starting at the bottom, outline and fill in the three alternate stripes on the tail.

Turquoise (3) *Short loop:* Outline and fill in the eyes (the eye buttons will be sewn on top of the turquoise yarn later, when you trim the cat).

Coral (4) *Short loop:* Outline and fill in the triangles inside the ears. Outline and fill in the nose. Punch down one row from the nose to the mouth. Then punch two rows across for the mouth.

Maroon (1) *Long loop:* Fill in the two remaining stripes in the tail. Outline the head and body and fill in all the bare areas.

Check for any skimpy spots and fill in if necessary.

See Chapter 11 for instructions for trimming your pillow, and Chapter 12 for finishing it.

1 Maroon
2 Lavender
3 Turquoise
4 Coral

Dog I

MATERIALS

Burlap: 16″ × 20″ (tape the edges)
Yarn: rust, 35 yards
medium brown, 40 yards
dark brown, 20 yards
black, 5 yards

TRIM

2 ¾-inch black leather eye buttons
1 1-inch black leather nose button

FOR FINISHING

Iron-on interfacing: 14″ × 18″
Backing: 16″ × 20″
Stuffing: ¾ pound polyester fiber

TRANSFERRING THE DESIGN

Leave a 2-inch margin on all sides and draw a grid of 2-inch squares, 8 squares high by 6 squares wide, with your blue felt marker.

Locate the nose and ears as key points on your grid. (The nose is an inverted black triangle with a button sewn on top.) Copy the rest of the design, square by square, from the illustration. Check against the centerline to make sure the sides are equal. Go over the final drawing with your black felt marker.

PUNCHING THE DESIGN

Black (4) *Short loop:* Outline and fill in the triangle of the nose.

Rust (1) *Long loop:* Outline and fill in the ears.

Medium brown (2) *Long loop:* Outline and fill in the chest below the whiskers, and the two front legs. *Short loop:* Outline and fill in the head between the ears. *Extra long loop:* (See page 28.) Punch the area between the nose and the ears to make whiskers, but loosely so that you will be able to add some dark brown punches later.

Dark brown (3) *Long loop:* Punch one row straight across the bottom. *Short loop:* Outline and fill in the body on the outside of each leg and between the legs. *Extra long loop:* Fill in the area of the whiskers with random punches to mix with the light brown extra long loops.

Check for any skimpy spots and fill in if necessary.

See Chapter 11 for instructions for trimming your pillow, and Chapter 12 for finishing it.

1 Rust
2 Medium brown
3 Dark brown
4 Black

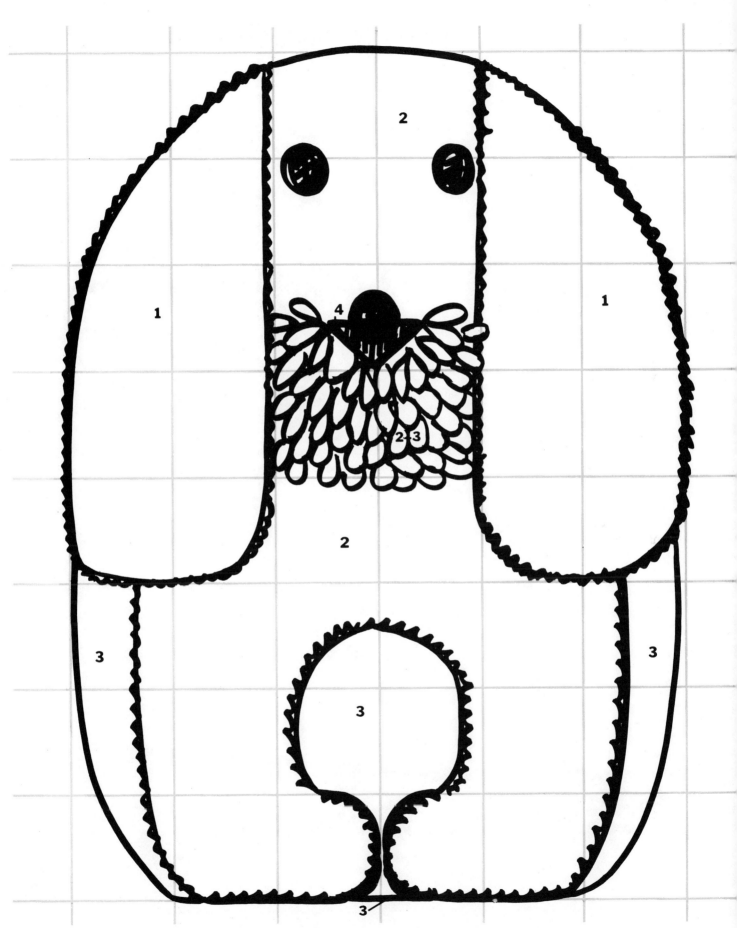

EACH SQUARE EQUALS 2 INCHES

Dog II, "Rover"

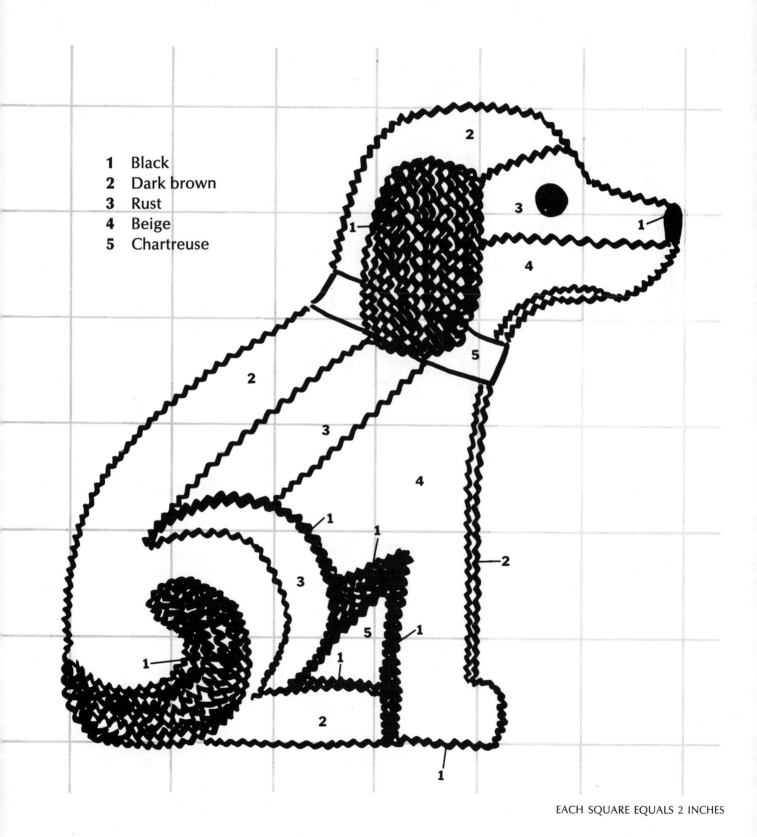

1 Black
2 Dark brown
3 Rust
4 Beige
5 Chartreuse

EACH SQUARE EQUALS 2 INCHES

MATERIALS

Burlap: 16″ × 16″ (tape the edges)
Yarn: black, 30 yards
  dark brown, 30 yards
  rust, 25 yards
  beige, 30 yards
  chartreuse, 5 yards

TRIM

1 black eye button

FOR FINISHING

Iron-on interfacing: 14″ × 14″
Backing: 16″ × 16″
Stuffing: ½ pound polyester fiber

TRANSFERRING THE DESIGN

Leave a 2-inch margin on all sides and draw a grid of 2-inch squares, 6 squares high by 6 squares wide, with your blue felt marker.

Locate the nose, the ear, the line of the front leg and the line of the back as key points on your grid. All the black-filled areas of the illustration are to be punched in black—there's no need for you to blacken them on your burlap. Copy the rest of the design, square by square, from the illustration. Go over the finished drawing with your black felt marker.

PUNCHING THE DESIGN

Black (1) *Long loop:* Outline and fill in the ears, the tail and the black area underneath the stomach. Punch one row to outline the upper curve of the back leg down across the top of the back foot. Punch one row down the back of the front leg and across underneath the front foot. *Short loop:* Outline and fill in the tip of the nose.

Dark brown (2) *Long loop:* Starting at the chin, punch two rows down the chest and the front leg to the top of the foot. Outline and fill in the top of the head and the back, including the back leg around the tail area and the back foot.

Rust (3) *Long loop:* Outline and fill in the middle of the head around the eye, the center section of the body, and the upper part of the back leg.

Beige (4) *Long loop:* Fill in the lower part of the head. Fill in the front of the body, below the collar, including the front leg and foot.

Chartreuse (5) *Short loop:* Outline and fill in the collar. Fill in the area between the stomach and the legs.

Check for any skimpy spots and fill in if necessary.

See Chapter 11 for instructions for trimming your pillow, and Chapter 12 for finishing it.

The Hen

MATERIALS

Burlap: 16″ × 24″ (tape the edges)
Yarn: bright red, 35 yards
  orange, 50 yards
  white, 35 yards
  yellow orange, 15 yards
  black, 25 yards

FOR FINISHING

Iron-on interfacing: 14″ × 22″
Backing: 16″ × 24″
Stuffing: 1 pound polyester fiber

TRANSFERRING THE DESIGN

Leave a 2-inch margin on all sides and draw a grid of 2-inch squares, 6 squares high and 10 squares wide, with your blue felt marker.

Locate the beak, the beginning of the wing and the top of the tail as key points on your grid. Copy the rest of the design, square by square, from the illustration. Don't worry if your zigzag lines vary slightly from those in the picture—it won't change the over-all effect. Round the bottom of the hen so that it extends slightly below the bottom line of your grid. Go over the final drawing with your black felt marker.

PUNCHING THE DESIGN

Black (5) *Long loop:* Outline the three sections of the wing and the three sections of the tail. Punch one row under the comb. Punch one row across the beak. *Short loop:* Punch the pupil of the eye.

Bright red (1) *Long loop:* Outline the comb and fill in. Fill in the top and bottom sections of the wing, and the outside and inside sections of the tail.

Yellow orange (4) *Long loop:* Fill in the center section of the wing and the center section of the tail. *Short loop:* Outline and fill in the beak. Punch the zigzag line on the neck. Then outline the bottom of the body from the zigzag line on the neck to the base of the tail.

Orange (2) *Short loop:* Outline and fill in the head, but leave the eyes bare for the moment. Outline and fill in the body above and around the wing, making sharp points where the zigzag line delineates the area.

White (3) *Short lopp:* Fill in the areas on the neck on either side of the zigzag line. Continue to fill in the outer area of the body between the orange points and the bottom line and the tail. Fill in the eye around the black pupil.

Check for any skimpy spots and fill in if necessary.

See Chapter 12 for instructions for finishing your pillow.

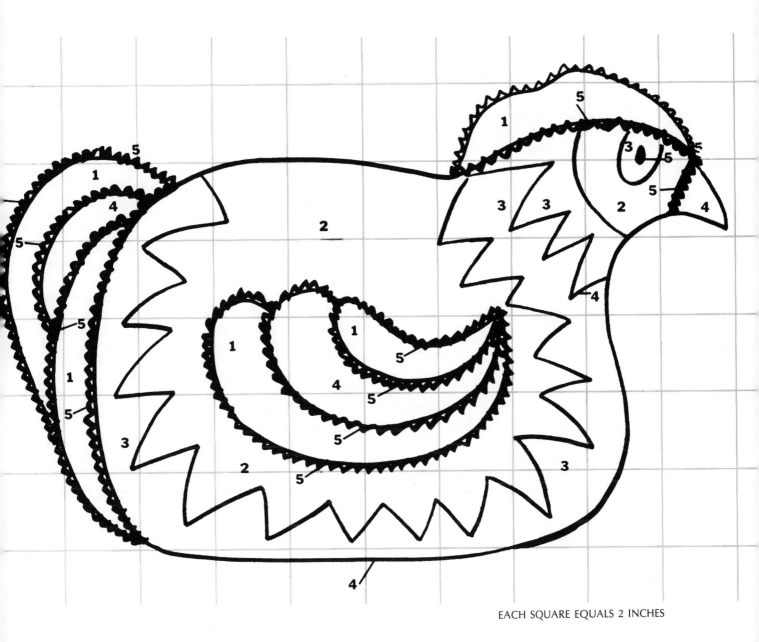

EACH SQUARE EQUALS 2 INCHES

1 Bright red
2 Orange
3 White
4 Yellow orange
5 Black

The Owl

MATERIALS

Burlap: 18″ × 16″ (tape the edges)
Yarn: black, 50 yards
medium brown, 35 yards
dark brown, 40 yards
grass green, 7 yards
yellow orange, 7 yards
lemon yellow, 2 yards

FOR FINISHING

Iron-on interfacing: 16″ × 14″
Backing: 18″ × 16″
Stuffing: ⅔ pound polyester fiber

TRANSFERRING THE DESIGN

Leave a 2-inch margin on all sides and draw a grid of 2-inch squares, 7 squares high by 6 squares wide, with your blue felt marker.

Locate the ears (they extend from the top of the wings slightly above the top of the grid), the point of the beak and the bottom of the wings as key points on your grid. Copy the rest of the design, square by square, from the illustration. Note that the scallops of the breast feathers follow the grid lines, except for the bottom row. Check against the centerline to make sure the sides are equal. Go over the final drawing with your black felt marker.

PUNCHING THE DESIGN

Black (1) *Long loop:* Outline and fill in the border of each wing. Outline the beak by punching one row from the tip of one ear down to the point in the center and up to the tip of the other ear. *Extra long loop:* Punch the ear loops from the top of each wing to the tip of each ear (see page 28). *Short loop:* Starting from the beak just above the pupil of each eye, punch four stitches down to make the pupil. Then outline the bottom of each scalloped row of feathers.

Medium brown (2) *Long loop:* Punch the line across the top of the head and fill in the area of the beak. *Short loop:* Fill in the scalloped areas of the feathers just above each black outline.

Dark brown (3) *Long loop:* Fill in the center of each wing. *Short loop:* Fill in the centers of the feather scallops. Fill in the triangular-shaped areas between the outer edge of the eyes and the wings and beak. Fill in the area below the eyes and above the first line of medium brown feathers.

Grass green (4) *Short loop:* Outline the outermost circle of the eyes and fill in.

Yellow orange (5) *Short loop:* Fill in the middle circle of each eye.

Lemon yellow (6) *Short loop:* Fill in the inner circle of each eye around the black-punched pupil.

Check for any skimpy spots and fill in if necessary.

See Chapter 12 for instructions for finishing your pillow.

1	Black
2	Medium brown
3	Dark brown
4	Grass green
5	Yellow orange
6	Lemon yellow

The Lion

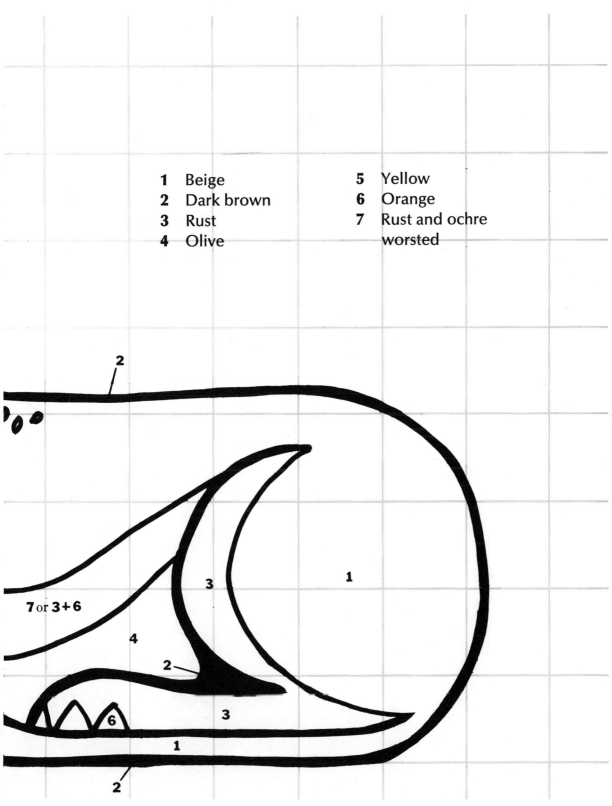

1	Beige	**5**	Yellow
2	Dark brown	**6**	Orange
3	Rust	**7**	Rust and ochre
4	Olive		worsted

EACH SQUARE EQUALS 2 INCHES

MATERIALS

Burlap: 28″ × 20″ (tape the edges)
Yarn: beige, 115 yards
    dark brown, 20 yards
    rust, 35 yards
    olive, 20 yards
    yellow, 4 yards
    orange, 10 yards
    rust and ochre worsted, 30 yards of each

TRIM

28 inches of dark brown upholstery fringe

FOR FINISHING

Iron-on interfacing: 26″ × 18″
Backing: 28″ × 20″
Stuffing: 1½ pounds polyester fiber

TRANSFERRING THE DESIGN

Leave a 2-inch margin on all sides and draw a grid of 2-inch squares, 12 squares wide by 8 squares high, with your blue felt marker.

Locate the ears, eyebrows, nose, cheeks, front paws and the back paw resting on the tail as key points on your grid. You don't need to draw the dotted lines around the head and the tip of the tail. They're not to be punched—they show where fringe is to be added later as trim. Copy the rest of the design, square by square, from the illustration.

PUNCHING THE DESIGN

Dark brown (2) *Long loop:* Punch the eyebrows. *Short loop:* Outline the outside of the entire lion—head, ears, back, rump, tail, back leg and front paws. Outline the nose and the round cheeks below it, but not the line of the jowls going up the side of the face.

Rust (3) *Short loop:* Outline and fill in the inside of each ear. Outline and fill loosely the spot in the center of the forehead. Punch two rows around to fill the outermost semicircle of each eye. Then punch one row down inside the dark brown outline of the nose on both sides, and one row around inside the dark brown outline of each cheek. Now fill the jowls on either side of the face, starting with one row up near the ears and widening to three rows at the bottom, where the jowls meet the cheeks. Fill the narrow area along the lower part of each front leg. Outline the zigzag inner border of the claws. Fill in the curve of the haunch and the back leg up to the claws.

Olive (4) *Short loop:* Punch three rows to fill the middle semicircle of each eye. Turn your burlap over. Working from the front, outline and fill in the area above and below the two front paws; the small triangular area below the nose between the two cheeks; and the area between the back leg, the underbelly and the front leg. Cut the yarn on the back.

Yellow (5) *Short loop:* Fill the triangular-shaped pupils of both eyes.

Orange (6) *Short loop:* Fill the muzzle at the tip of the nose. Fill the inside of the claws on the front and back feet. (See the Note under Materials.)

Beige (1) *Short loop:* Fill in the head. Fill in the

upper part of each front leg, the back, the rump and the tail.

Rust and ochre worsted (7) *Long loop:* Use one ball of rust worsted and one of ochre worsted. Thread a strand from each through your punch needle (see page 18). Punch a few loops through the spot in the middle of the forehead and several loops along the top of the back, where indicated, for tufts. *Short loop:* Fill in the area just beneath the head, between the upper part of the two front legs. Fill in the underbelly.

NOTE: If you prefer not to use the worsted yarns, you can punch all the rust and ochre areas with rust rug-and-craft yarn loosely, and then fill them in with random loops of orange. The long loop tufts can be punched with the rust alone. The whisker trim (see page 151) can also be made of rust yarn instead of rust and ochre worsted.

Check for any skimpy spots and fill in if necessary.

See Chapter 11 for instructions for trimming your pillow, and Chapter 12 for finishing it.

The Parrot
(The Roseate Cockatoo)

MATERIALS

Burlap: 14″ × 20″ (tape the edges)
Yarn: light pink, 17 yards
dark pink, 27 yards
lavender, 15 yards
gray, 35 yards
black, 17 yards
maroon, 15 yards
white, 1 yard

TRIM

1 round shiny black eye button

FOR FINISHING

Iron-on interfacing: 12″ × 18″
Backing: 14″ × 20″
Stuffing: ⅔ pound polyester fiber

TRANSFERRING THE DESIGN

Leave a 2-inch margin on all sides and draw a grid of 2-inch squares, 8 squares high by 5 squares wide, with your blue felt marker.

Locate the beak, the cheek and the curve of the chest as key points on your grid. Copy the rest of the design, square by square, from the illustration. Go over the final drawing with your black felt marker.

PUNCHING THE DESIGN

(NOTE: *The entire design is punched in short loop.*)

Black (5): Outline the beak. Outline the two wings and each individual feather in both. Outline both claws and the rounded edge of the tail.

Gray (4): Fill in the beak. Fill in the claws. Then fill in all the feathers in both wings except the three where lavender is indicated.

Lavender (3): Fill in the three remaining feathers in the wings. Outline and fill in the base.

Maroon (6): Outline and fill in the area just under the beak. Outline and fill in the area beside the cheek. Outline and fill in the area above the right claw, the area between the two claws, and the area in the tail.

Dark pink (2): Outline and fill in the cheek. Outline and fill in the three feathers in the second row of feathers across the breast. Outline and fill in the fourth and the sixth rows of feathers across the breast (the intervening rows will be filled in with light pink). Fill in the area at the bottom of the tail, just above the black outline. Fill lower body.

Light pink (1): Outline and fill in the top of the head. Outline and fill in the two feathers at the top of the breast. Then fill in the breast feathers in the alternate rows between the dark pink rows.

White (7): Working from the front, fill in the eye. Cut the yarn on the back.

Check for any skimpy spots and fill in if necessary.

See Chapter 11 for instructions for trimming your pillow, and Chapter 12 for finishing it.

1	Light pink	**5**	Black
2	Dark pink	**6**	Maroon
3	Lavender	**7**	White
4	Gray		

EACH SQUARE EQUALS 2 INCHES

The Green Cheeked Amazon

EACH SQUARE EQUALS 2 INCHES

You can turn the Roseate Cockatoo into a Green Cheeked Amazon by simply using a different set of colored yarns. You'll need a good bright red for the top of the head, the edge of the wings and around the tail, and three shades of green instead of two shades of pink for the body feathers. Measurements for each of the different colored yarns you'll need, as well as a revised color code, are given below. Punch the design according to the color code keyed on the illustration. (This version faces in the opposite direction so that you can punch both parrots if you like and set the pillows facing each other.) Remember, the entire design is punched in short loop. And you can also outline the beak, claws and wing feathers with the royal blue.

Yarn: grass green, 25 yards
 royal blue, 26 yards
 forest green, 23 yards
 dark olive, 15 yards
 straw, 7 yards
 red, 10 yards
 white, 1 yard

1 Grass green
2 Royal blue
3 Forest green
4 Dark olive
5 Straw
6 Red
7 White

CHAPTER

7

THE FISH

The sleek shape of fish make them a perfect subject for punch pillows. They swim happily across the top of a couch or a window seat.

The Holy Mackerel and the Get-Well Cod are not really as complicated as they look. Because they were designed to allow the bare burlap to show through their scales, the punching proceeds quite quickly. Although the Loan Shark and the Pin-Striped Bass look easier, they actually take longer to make because they are punched solid.

The Mermaid is really a combination fish and people pillow. Both her skin and her scales are punched solid, so she, too, takes a little longer to make—but I think she's worth it!

The Holy Mackerel

MATERIALS

Burlap: yellow, 16″ × 24″ (tape the edges)
Yarn: yellow, 45 yards
   yellow orange, 30 yards
   royal blue, 35 yards
   dark green, 50 yards
   wine, 15 yards

TRIM

1 shiny yellow eye button

FOR FINISHING

Iron-on interfacing: 14″ × 22″
Backing: 16″ × 24″
Stuffing: 1 pound polyester fiber

TRANSFERRING THE DESIGN

Leave a 2-inch margin on all sides and draw a grid of 2-inch squares, 6 squares high by 10 squares wide, with your blue felt marker.

Locate the curving line that separates the face from the body and the fin in the center of the body as key points on your grid. Copy the rest of the design, square by square, from the illustration. The scales don't have to be exactly the same as those in the design, but draw them so that each row forms a continuous scalloped line from the top of the body down to the bottom. That way they'll be easier to punch. Go over the finished drawing with your black felt marker.

PUNCHING THE DESIGN

Dark green (4) *Long loop:* Outline the three fins —top, center and bottom—and the tail. Punch the two rows within each fin that separate the three sections from each other, and the four rows within the tail that separate its five sections. Punch the inner circle around the pupil of the eye. Punch the first of the three curving vertical lines separating the head from the body, the first of the three vertical lines at the back of the tail and the first of the three vertical lines at the back of each fin. *Short loop:* Skip the first scalloped line of the scales and punch the outline of the second. Stop when you reach the fin and cut the yarn on the right side; then complete the outline on the opposite side of the fin to the end. Punch the fourth outline in the same way. Continue punching alternate outlines of scales until you reach the tail.

Royal blue (3) *Long loop:* Punch the outer circle around the eye. Punch the second vertical curving line separating the head from the body, and the second vertical line at the back of each fin and at the back of the tail. *Short loop:* Punch the mouth. Punch the outline of the first scalloped line of the scales. Punch the third and the fifth in the same way. Continue punching the alternate outlines between the green outlines until you reach the tail. (The burlap between the blue and green scale outlines remains bare.)

Wine (5) *Long loop:* Punch the third curving vertical line separating the head from the body, the third vertical line at the back of each fin and the third line at the back of the tail. Fill in the center section in the tail. *Short loop:* Fill in the center of the eye.

Yellow (1) *Short loop:* Punch each of the lines that curve down the face. Fill in the center section of the center fin, and the center section of the upper and the lower fins. Fill in the two sections of the tail on either side of the center section.

Yellow orange (2) *Short loop:* Fill in the face. Fill in the two outer sections within each fin, and the two outer sections of the tail.

Check for any skimpy spots and fill in if necessary.

See Chapter 11 for instructions for trimming your pillow, and Chapter 12 for finishing it.

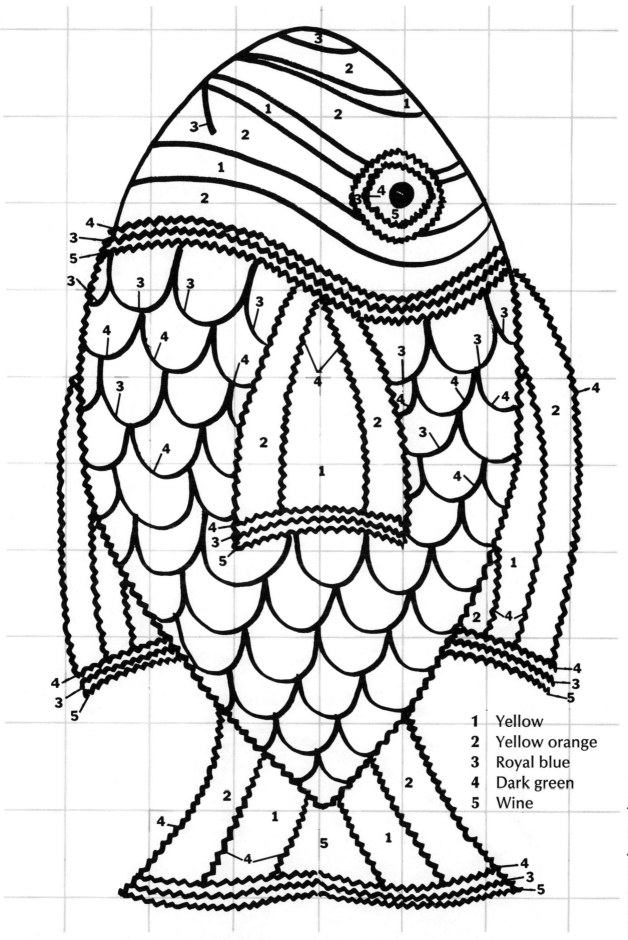

1 Yellow
2 Yellow orange
3 Royal blue
4 Dark green
5 Wine

The Loan Shark

MATERIALS

Burlap: 32″ × 14″ (tape the edges)
Yarn: navy blue, 60 yards
 red, 40 yards
 orange, 40 yards
 white, 4 yards

TRIM

1 shiny gold eye button

FOR FINISHING

Iron-on interfacing: 30″ × 12″
Backing: 32″ × 14″
Stuffing: 1 pound polyester fiber

TRANSFERRING THE DESIGN

Leave a 2-inch margin on all sides and draw a grid of 2-inch squares, 14 squares long by 5 squares high, with your blue felt marker.

Locate the tip of the nose, the tip of the tail, the tip of the fins, and the points where the body is widest and narrowest as key points on your grid. Draw a sweeping curved line to get the top and bottom outline of the fish. Copy the rest of the design, square by square, from the illustration. Go over the final drawing with your black felt marker.

PUNCHING THE DESIGN

Navy blue (1) *Long loop:* Outline and fill in the top section of the body from the tail straight across to the head. Outline and fill in the top section of the upper fin and the bottom section of the two lower fins. Outline and fill in the bottom area on the

tail. *Short loop:* Punch one row for each of the three stripes of the gills just behind the mouth.

Red (2) *Long loop:* Outline and fill in the second section across the body that divides at the tail, but leave the eye bare for the moment. Outline and fill in the second section in each of the three fins. *Short loop:* The third section of the body is a mixture of red and orange. Fill this area loosely with haphazard punches, leaving room to add orange. Use the same technique for the center area of the tail and the three remaining sections of the fins. Working from the front, punch one row for the zigzag line of the teeth.

Orange (3) *Short loop:* Outline and fill in the bottom section of the body, except the mouth. Now punch the third section of the body with haphazard punches until it is thoroughly mixed with the red and completely filled. Do the same thing in the center area of the tail and the three sections of the fins that were loosely punched with red.

White (4) *Short loop:* Working from the front, first fill in the eye area, and then the teeth above and below the red zigzag line.

Check for any skimpy spots and fill in if necessary.

See Chapter 11 for instructions for trimming your pillow, and Chapter 12 for finishing it.

1 Navy blue
2 Red
3 Orange
4 White

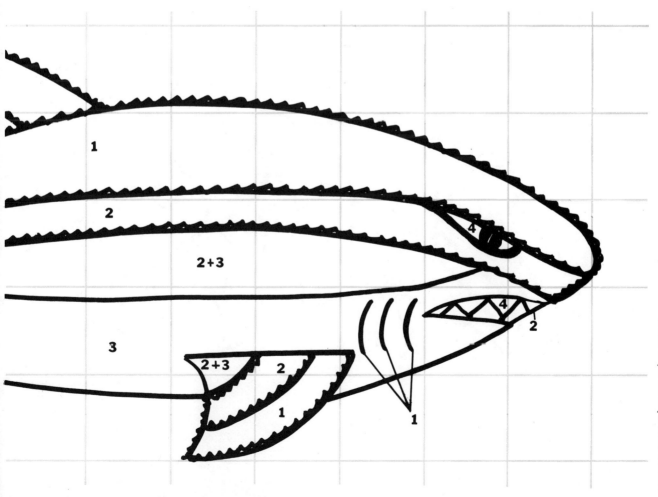

EACH SQUARE EQUALS 2 INCHES

The Mermaid

MATERIALS

    Burlap: 16″ × 32″ (tape the edges)
    Yarn: dark green, 40 yards
          chartreuse, 40 yards
          emerald green, 40 yards
          old rose, 40 yards
          hot pink, 10 yards
          purple, 25 yards

TRIM

    1 small red heart-shaped mouth button
    1 small pink nose button
    2 small pearl breast buttons

FOR FINISHING

    Iron-on interfacing: 14″ × 30″
    Backing: green, 16″ × 32″
    Stuffing: 1⅓ pounds polyester fiber

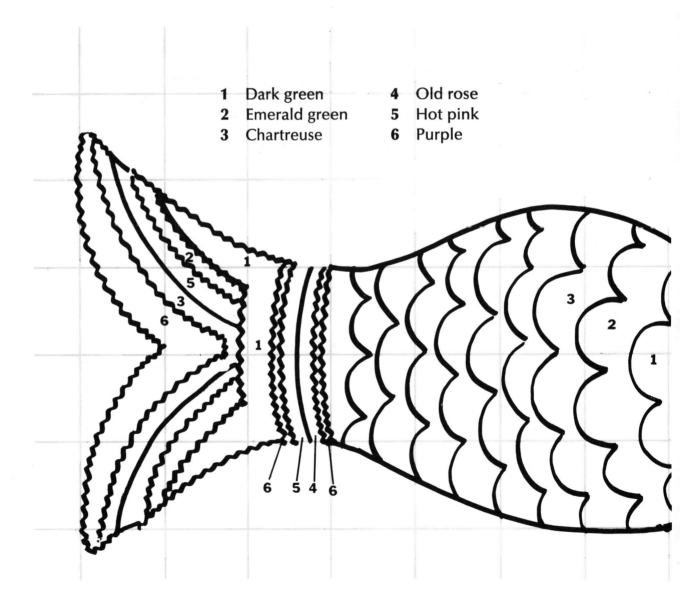

1 Dark green   **4** Old rose
2 Emerald green   **5** Hot pink
3 Chartreuse   **6** Purple

TRANSFERRING THE DESIGN

Leave a 2-inch margin on all sides and draw a grid of 2-inch squares, 6 squares high by 14 squares long, with your blue felt marker.

Locate the outline of the hair, the band at the waist and the band separating the body from the tail as key points on your grid. Draw a sweeping line to get the curve of the hair and hips. Copy the rest of the design, square by square, from the illustration. The scales don't have to be exactly like those in the picture, but loop them down the body in rows so

that they'll be easy to punch. Go over the final drawing with your black felt marker.

PUNCHING THE DESIGN

Dark green (1) *Long loop:* Punch the outside section of the hair on both sides of the face. Fill the area at the beginning of the tail, just after the band of stripes. *Short loop:* Fill the area at the bottom between the hair and the waistline. Fill in the first row

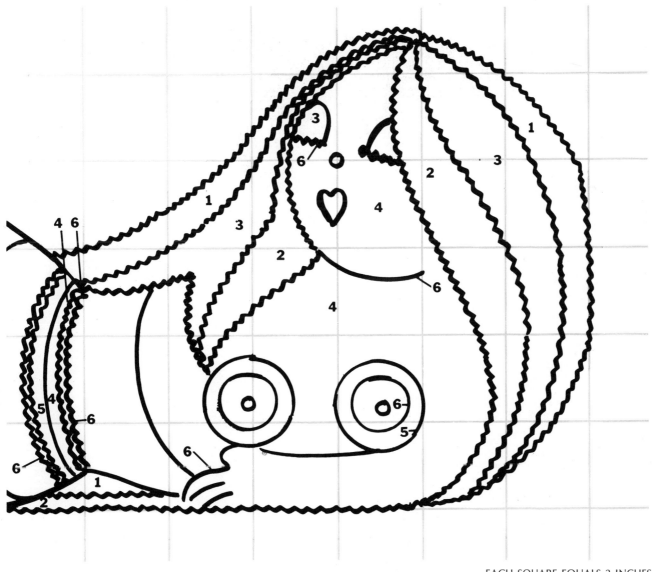

EACH SQUARE EQUALS 2 INCHES

of scales from top to bottom; then fill in the fourth, seventh and tenth rows.

Emerald green (2) *Long loop:* Punch the inside section of the hair on both sides of the face, and the hair on the bottom below the waist. Punch two rows along both sides of the tail next to the dark green. *Short loop:* Fill in the second row of scales from top to bottom; then fill in the fifth and eighth rows.

Chartreuse (3) *Long loop:* Fill in the middle sections of the hair on both sides of the face. Fill in the second to last section in the tail. *Short loop:* Fill in the third row of scales from top to bottom; then fill in the sixth and ninth rows. Fill in the eyelids.

Purple (6) *Long loop:* Punch one row of eyelashes under each eyelid. Punch two rows at the beginning and two rows at the end of the waist band and the band separating the body from the tail. Fill in the last section of the tail. *Short loop:* Outline the chin and the two arms, including the fingers. Punch the inner circle around the breasts.

Hot pink (5) *Short loop:* Punch the outer circle around the breasts. Punch two rows next to the purple at the end of the band at the waistline and at the end of the band near the tail. Punch the two areas in the middle of the tail between the emerald green and the chartreuse sections.

Old rose (4) *Short loop:* Fill in the face and body areas. Punch two rows between the first two rows of purple and the hot pink in the band at the waistline and in the band near the tail.

Check for any skimpy spots and fill in, if necessary.

See chapter 11 for instructions for trimming your pillow, and Chapter 12 for finishing it.

The Get-Well Cod

MATERIALS

Burlap: forest green, 32″ × 14″ (tape the edges)
Yarn: sky blue, 35 yards
　　　turquoise, 12 yards
　　　royal blue, 25 yards
　　　purple, 25 yards
　　　wine, 18 yards
　　　lemon yellow, 25 yards

TRIM

1 flat round pearly yellow eye button

FOR FINISHING

Iron-on interfacing: 30″ × 12″
Backing: 32″ × 14″
Stuffing: 1 pound polyester fiber

TRANSFERRING THE DESIGN

Leave a 2-inch margin on all sides and draw a grid of 2-inch squares, 14 squares long by 5 squares high, with your blue felt marker.

Locate the two bands with the zigzag lines as key points on your grid (note that the band next to the head curves while the band on the tail is straight), as well as the fin and the diamond-shaped section of the tail. Copy the rest of the design, square by square, from the illustration. The scales don't have to be exactly the same as pictured—just make sure they loop down the body in rows so that they'll be easy to punch. Go over the final drawing with your black felt marker.

PUNCHING THE DESIGN

Purple (4) *Long loop:* Punch the inside row on either side of the zigzag band at the tip of the tail and the zigzag band between the head and the body.

Punch the inner outline of the fin and then the horizontal row through its center. Punch the inside row on either side of the diamond-shaped inset at the beginning of the tail and the crossed lines inside the diamond. Punch the outside ring around the eye. *Short loop:* Punch the line of the mouth.

Royal blue (3) *Long loop:* Punch the outside row on either side of each of the two zigzag bands. Punch the outline of the fin just outside of the purple outline. Punch the inner ring around the eye. *Short loop:* Counting from the head to the tail, punch the third scalloped outline of the scales. When you reach the fin, cut the yarn on the front and start up again on the other side until you complete the row. Punch the sixth row of scales the same way, and then the ninth row (where you're no longer interrupted by the fin). Punch the third row of scales in the tail area.

Wine (5) *Short loop:* Outline and fill in the triangles in the two zigzag bands—the five nearest the face in the first band, and the three in the tail in the second band. Fill in the center of the eye. Fill in the four sections surrounding the diamond inset in the area at the beginning of the tail.

Turquoise (2) *Short loop:* Punch the five rows that curve down the face, skipping the eye area and the line of the mouth. Now proceed to the scales and punch the second row down. Stop when you reach the fin and cut the yarn on the right side; then continue down the rest of the scalloped line. Do the same thing with the fifth row. Then punch the eighth and the eleventh rows of scales in the body, and the second row of scales in the tail section.

Sky blue (1) *Short loop:* Outline the face and fill in the areas between the turquoise lines and around the eye. Outline top and bottom the two areas of the body where the scales are, between the three dividing bands. Then punch the first row of scales down. Stop at the fin and cut the yarn on the right side. Start again on the other side of the fin and continue down the rest of the scalloped line. Punch the fourth and seventh rows the same way; then punch the tenth row, and the first row of scales in the tail area.

Lemon yellow (6) *Short loop:* Fill the inside of

the fin on both sides of the horizontal purple line. Fill the four areas of the diamond-shaped inset between the crossed purple lines. Now fill the four remaining triangles in each of the two zigzag bands.

The area between the rows of scales remains bare so that the green burlap shows through. Check the rest of your design for any skimpy areas and fill in if necessary.

See Chapter 11 for instructions for trimming your pillow, and Chapter 12 for finishing it.

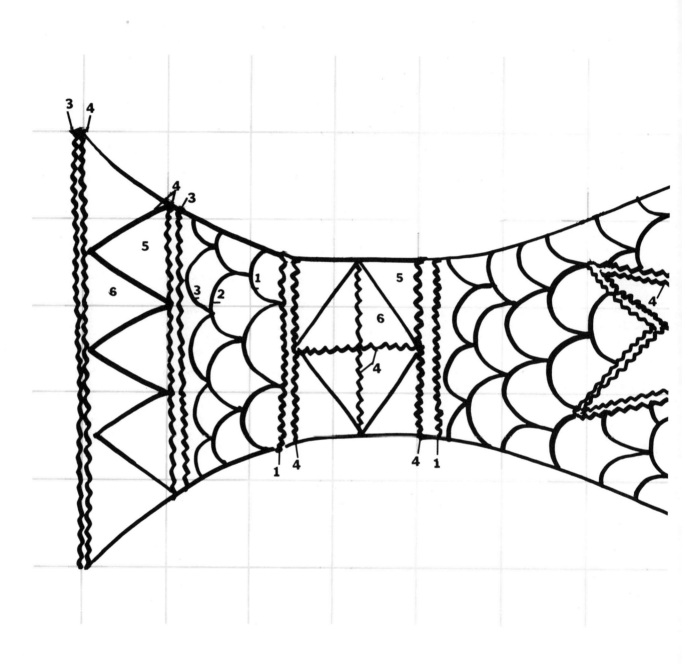

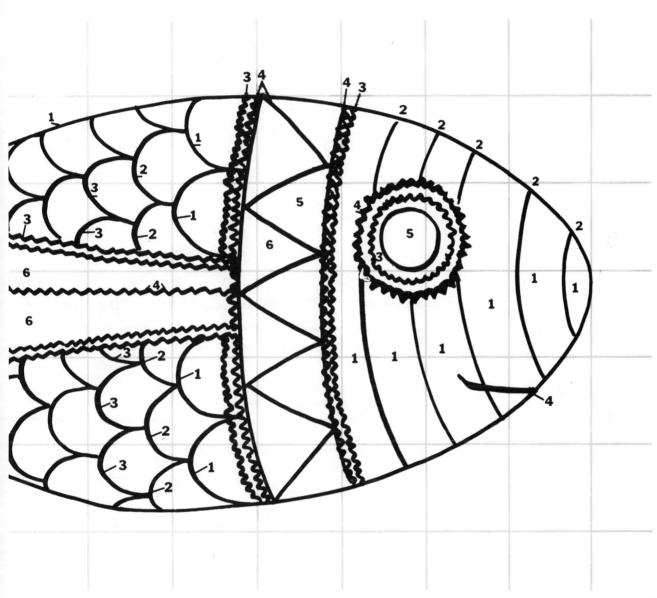

EACH SQUARE EQUALS 2 INCHES

1	Sky blue	4	Purple
2	Turquoise	5	Wine
3	Royal blue	6	Lemon yellow

The Pin-Striped Bass

MATERIALS

Burlap: 18″ × 34″ (tape the edges)
Yarn: black, 75 yards
      light gray, 65 yards
      dark gray, 35 yards
      white, 20 yards

TRIM

1 shiny round red eye button

FOR FINISHING

Iron-on interfacing: 16″ × 32″
Backing: 18″ × 34″
Stuffing: 1½ pounds polyester fiber

1 Black
2 Light gray
3 Dark gray
4 White

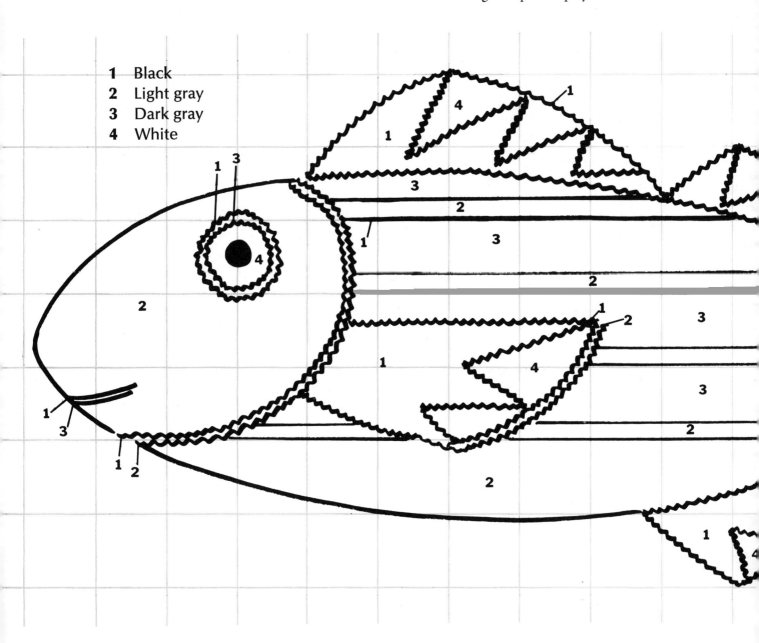

TRANSFERRING THE DESIGN

Leave a 2-inch margin on all sides and draw a grid of 2-inch squares, 7 squares high by 15 squares long, with your blue felt marker.

Locate the curving line that separates the head from the body, the fins and the tail as key points on your grid. Copy the rest of the design, square by square, from the illustration. Note that the four black stripes that cross the body horizontally fol-

low the grid lines, and that the light gray lines are directly above them. Go over the final drawing with your black felt marker.

PUNCHING THE DESIGN

Black (1) *Long loop:* Punch the outer circle around the eye. Punch the first line separating the head from the body. Outline all four fins and the tail (an extra row of light gray will be added at the back of the center fin and the back of the tail later). Punch the middle row inside the tail area, and then fill in the area between that line and the zigzag line in the tail. Fill in the areas inside the zigzag lines in the four fins, as indicated. *Short loop:* Punch the upper line of the mouth. Then punch one row along each grid line in the body to get four horizontal black stripes (as indicated).

Light gray (2) *Long loop:* Punch the second line separating the head from the body. Punch one row at the back of the center fin and one row at the back of the tail. *Short loop:* Outline the head and fill in, except for the eye and the bottom line of the mouth. Fill in the band at the beginning of the tail. Punch two horizontal rows just above each horizontal black line running across the body. Then outline the bottom of the body from the head to the bottom fin, and fill the area of the body above it up to the bottom black horizontal line.

Dark gray (3) *Long loop:* Punch another circle around the eye, just inside the black circle. *Short loop:* Punch the lower line of the mouth. Fill in the rest of the body between the horizontal lines.

White (4) *Short loop:* Fill in the center of the eye. Fill in the remaining bare areas of the fins and the tail on the outside of the zigzag lines.

Check for any skimpy areas and fill in if necessary.

See Chapter 11 for instructions for trimming your pillow, and Chapter 12 for finishing it.

VARIATIONS

It's easy to change the color scheme of the Pin-Striped Bass. If you prefer, you can substitute three shades of blue or three shades of green for the black and the two grays, and pale yellow for the white.

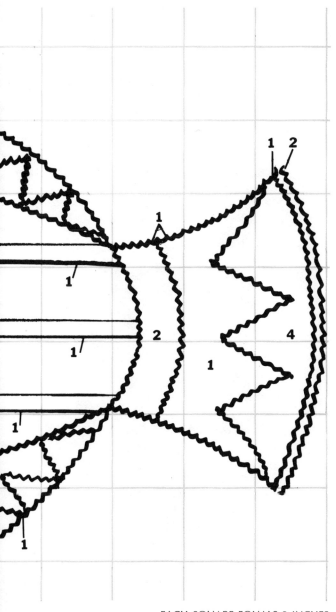

EACH SQUARE EQUALS 2 INCHES

CHAPTER

8

THE MONSTERS

Punch pillows don't have to be based on familiar, everyday creatures. They can be fearsome animals of our time such as the Rattlesnake in this chapter, or prehistoric beasts such as Sexy Rexy Tyrannosaurus and Dmitri Dimetrodon. They can even be creatures from Outer Space—for punching tames them all.

Manny, Moe and Max, incidentally—the three Little Creatures from Outer Space—could just as easily be called Myrtle, Maude and Mabel for anyone who prefers to think of space persons as female rather than male. Whatever their sex, they are among the simpler designs in the book— easy to copy onto your burlap and easy to punch. Chiefly because of its size, the Rattlesnake will probably take you the longest amount of time to make.

As always, of course, you're free to alter any of the designs to suit your fancy, as well as to create your own monsters to punch.

Sexy Rexy Tyrannosaurus

MATERIALS

Burlap: 22″ × 26″ (tape the edges)
Yarn: lavender, 50 yards
     turquoise, 30 yards
     peacock blue, 25 yards
     purple, 30 yards
     lemon yellow, 5 yards

FOR FINISHING

Iron-on interfacing: 20″ × 24″
Backing: 22″ × 26″
Stuffing: ¾ pound polyester fiber

TRANSFERRING THE DESIGN

Leave a 2-inch margin on all sides and draw a grid of 2-inch squares, 9 squares wide by 11 squares high, with your blue felt marker.

Locate the eye, the mouth, the arm, the leg and the bulge of the belly as key points on your grid. Copy the rest of the design, square by square, from the illustration. Go over the final drawing with your black felt marker.

PUNCHING THE DESIGN

Purple (4) *Long loop:* Punch one row all the way down the back, from above the eye to the tip of the tail. Punch three loops for the nostril. *Short loop:* Outline and fill in the bands at the top and bottom of the arm, the bands at the top and bottom of the leg and the band at the tip of the tail. Don't fill in the fingernails.

Peacock blue (3) *Short loop:* Outline and fill in the extra wide bands behind the arm and the leg. Outline and fill in the band near the end of the tail. Punch three loops for the center of the eye.

Turquoise (2) *Short loop:* Outline and fill in the band at the top of the body, just below the head, and the band just below the arm. Outline and fill in the band behind the top of the leg, the band at the bottom of the leg and the third band from the end of the tail.

Lavender (1) *Short loop:* Outline and fill in the head, but leave the teeth bare for the moment. Fill in the bands in the middle of the arm and the leg, the band in the middle of the belly, and the band near the tail. Outline and fill in the foot, but leave the nails bare as they will be filled in later with lemon yellow.

Lemon yellow (5) *Short loop:* Outline and fill in the eye around the peacock blue center. Fill in the teeth and the fingernails and toenails.

Check for any skimpy spots and fill in if necessary.

See Chapter 12 for instructions for finishing your pillow.

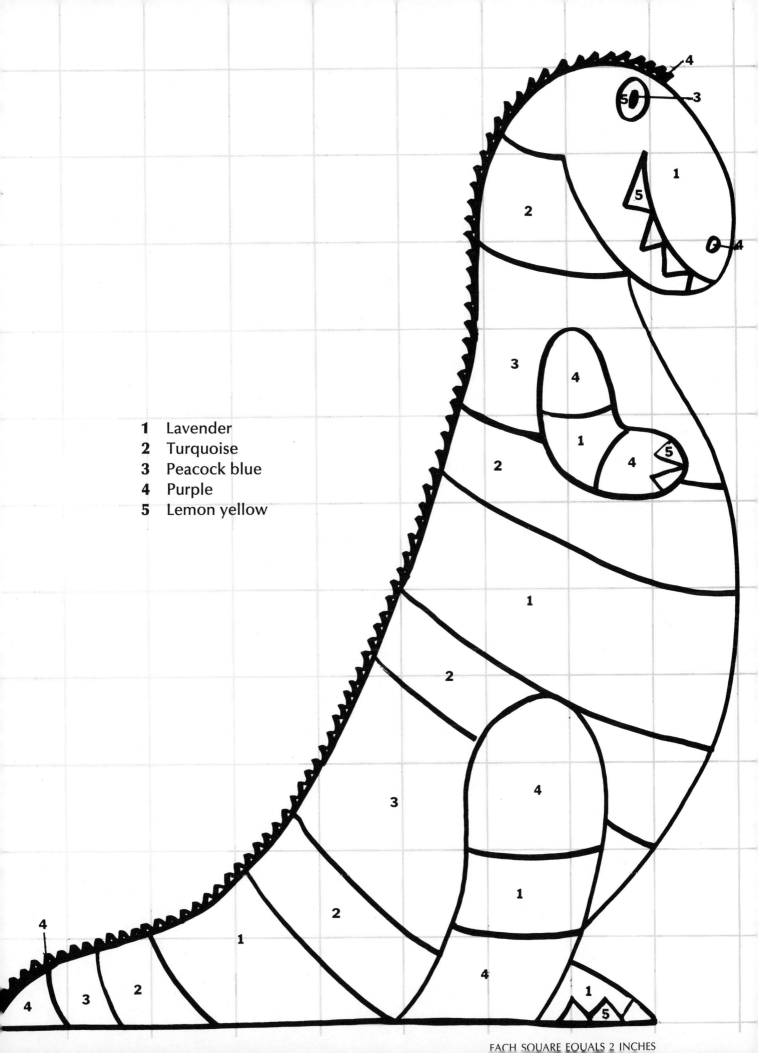

1 Lavender
2 Turquoise
3 Peacock blue
4 Purple
5 Lemon yellow

EACH SQUARE EQUALS 2 INCHES

Dmitri Dimetrodon

MATERIALS

Burlap: 26″ × 14″ (tape the edges)
Yarn: dark green, 40 yards
    olive, 35 yards
    chartreuse, 25 yards
    fuschia, 10 yards
    lemon yellow, 15 yards

FOR FINISHING

Iron-on interfacing: 24″ × 12″
Backing: 26″ × 14″
Stuffing: ½ pound polyester fiber

TRANSFERRING THE DESIGN

Leave a 2-inch margin on all sides and draw a grid of 2-inch squares, 11 squares wide by 5 squares high, with your blue felt marker.

Locate the beginning and end of the back fin, the line of the back and the legs as key points on your grid. Copy the rest of the design, square by square, from the illustration. Note that all the long loop vertical lines in the fin are on grid lines. Go over the final drawing with your black felt marker.

PUNCHING THE DESIGN

(NOTE: The freckles on the back, tail, legs and fin are punched after everything else. Don't worry

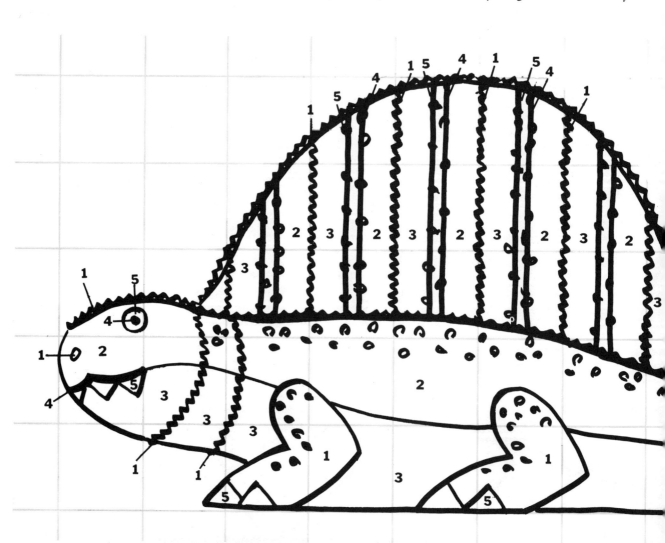

about leaving room for them. You can punch through the short loops with long loops later.)

Dark green (1) *Long loop:* Outline the back from the top of the head to the end of the tail. Outline the fin. Punch one row down each of the six vertical lines in the fin on the grid lines to make the spines of the fin. Punch the two lines around the neck. *Short loop:* Outline and fill in both legs but leave the toenails bare for the moment. Punch three loops for the nostril.

Olive (2) *Short loop:* Fill in the upper half of the head except for the eye. Fill in the upper half of the body all the way to the tail. Punch three vertical rows just to the left of each dark green vertical line in the fin.

Fuschia (4) *Short loop:* Punch one row just to the left of the olive rows in the fin. Punch one row

for the line of the mouth. Make three punches for the center of the eye.

Lemon yellow (5) *Short loop:* Punch one row alongside each row of fuschia in the fin. Fill in the eye around the fuschia center. Fill in the teeth and the toenails.

Chartreuse (3) *Short loop:* Outline and fill in the lower half of the head and body. Fill the remaining areas in the fin with vertical rows.

The freckles. *Long loop:* Use lemon yellow (5) first and punch haphazardly across the top of the back, the tail and the upper part of the legs. Change to fuschia (4) and do the same thing. Then take dark green (1) and punch a few haphazard loops on top of the fuschia and the yellow spines of the back fin. (NOTE: Don't make too many freckles—if you have, pull some of them out from the back.)

Check for any skimpy spots and fill in if necessary.

See Chapter 12 for instructions for finishing your pillow.

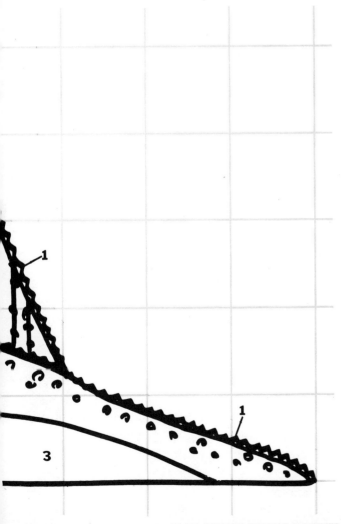

1   Dark green
2   Olive
3   Chartreuse
4   Fuschia
5   Lemon yellow

EACH SQUARE EQUALS 2 INCHES

The Rattlesnake

MATERIALS

Burlap: 54″ × 12″ (tape the edges)
Yarn: black, 25 yards
    rust, 30 yards
    ochre, 70 yards
    cream, 120 yards
    red, 15 yards

TRIM

2 small round red eye buttons
1 baby's rattle for the tail
red yarn tongue

FOR FINISHING

Iron-on interfacing: 54″ × 12″
Backing: cream or ochre, 8″ × 10″
Stuffing: styrofoam pellets

TRANSFERRING THE DESIGN

Leave a 2-inch margin on all sides and draw a grid of 2-inch squares, 25 squares long by 4 squares wide, with your blue felt marker.

Locate the oval in the center of the head as a key point on your grid. Then draw the eye patterns on either side of the oval, and the mouth pattern beneath it. Copy the rest of the design, square by square, from the illustration. Note that each of the large diamond shapes down the center of the back is two squares wide and two squares long. The small diamonds on the sides fit between the large ones. Continue drawing on your grid to make the body of your snake seven large diamonds long, plus the half-diamond that leads into the rattle pattern. Then add on the tail by copying the rattle pattern from the illustration. Go over the final drawing with your black felt marker.

PUNCHING THE DESIGN

It's easier to punch the snake if you approach it a section at a time, starting with the head and working your way down to the tail or rattles.

THE HEAD

Black (1) *Short loop:* Outline the round head inside the over-all outline of the snake that leads toward the first large center diamond of the body. Outline the two small diamonds inside the head, the two large loops above the eyes on either side of the center oval, and the mouth in the center below. Do not outline the center oval. Outline and fill in the two curved areas leading to the eyes.

Red (5) *Short loop:* Fill in the center of the two small diamonds. Outline and fill in the lower part of the mouth.

Cream (4) *Short loop:* Outline and fill in the center oval. Fill in the areas on either side of the mouth, then fill in the eyes.

Ochre (3) *Short loop:* Fill in the two large loops above the eyes and the upper part of the mouth.

Rust (2) *Short loop:* Fill in the area of the head around the central oval and the two small diamonds leading down into the first large diamond of the body.

THE DIAMONDS

Black (1) *Short loop:* Outline the first, third, fifth and seventh center diamonds with two rows. Outline the second, fourth, sixth and final half-diamonds with one row.

Ochre (3) *Short loop:* Outline and fill in all the side diamonds, including the two half-diamonds nearest the head.

Cream (4) *Short loop:* Punch two rows just inside the single row of black outlining each of the even-numbered diamonds including the final half-diamond. Then fill the entire background from the area around the head all the way down to the tail.

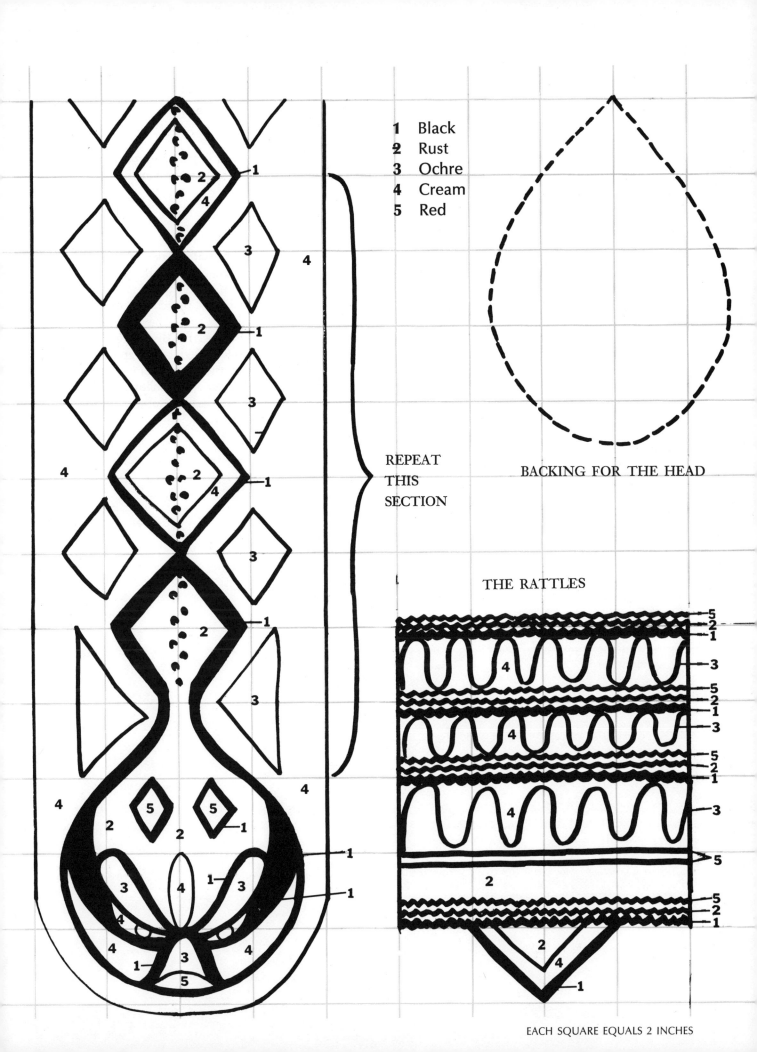

1 Black
2 Rust
3 Ochre
4 Cream
5 Red

REPEAT
THIS
SECTION

BACKING FOR THE HEAD

THE RATTLES

EACH SQUARE EQUALS 2 INCHES

Rust (2) *Short loop:* Fill in the inside of all the center diamonds.

Red (5) *Long loop:* Punch random stitches down the center of the large diamonds from the head to the tail. (This is indicated by the dots in the diamonds.)

THE RATTLES

Black (1) *Long loop:* Punch one row across at the end of the last half-diamond. Punch one row across at the end of each of the wavy lines.

Rust (2) *Long loop:* Punch one row across just after each of the rows of long loop black. *Short loop:* Fill in the first band of the tail.

Red (5) *Long loop:* Punch one row across just after each of the rows of long loop rust. *Short loop:* Punch two rows across just after the short loop band of rust.

Ochre (3) *Long loop:* Punch the three wavy lines.

Cream (4) *Short loop:* Fill in the background area around the wavy lines.

Check for any skimpy spots and fill in if necessary.

See Chapter 11 for instructions for trimming your pillow, and Chapter 12 for finishing it.

VARIATIONS

You can make the Rattlesnake as long as you like by adding more diamonds, although the 50 inches given here make this one quite formidable. You may also want to vary the colors, to make your snake more uniquely yours. The snake in the color photograph was punched by Miss Margery Schwartz of San Francisco. She used a dark and a light rust, punched cream in the ochre diamonds and didn't bother to be too exact about following the lines of the design. The result is a one-of-a-kind snake with a great deal of vitality.

Little Creatures from Outer Space: Manny

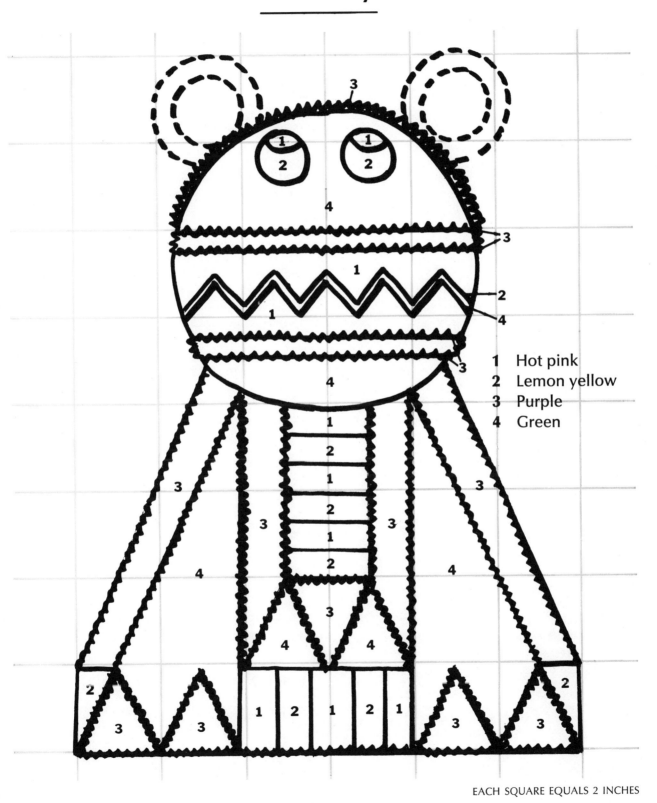

1 Hot pink
2 Lemon yellow
3 Purple
4 Green

EACH SQUARE EQUALS 2 INCHES

MATERIALS

Burlap: 16″ × 20″ (tape the edges)
Yarn: hot pink, 15 yards
　　　lemon yellow, 15 yards
　　　purple, 45 yards
　　　green, 37 yards

TRIM

2 bright brass curtain rings (with or without knobs)

FOR FINISHING

Iron-on interfacing: 14″ × 18″
Backing: 16″ × 20″
Stuffing: ½ pound polyester fiber

TRANSFERRING THE DESIGN

Leave a 2-inch margin on all sides and draw a grid of 2-inch squares, 6 squares wide by 8 squares high, with your blue felt marker.

Locate the zigzag line of the teeth, the outline of the head and the eyes as key points on your grid. The dotted line circles indicate the placement of the brass curtain rings for the antennae—you don't have to draw them on your burlap. The easiest way to copy Manny is to draw his head with a compass and his body with a ruler. Note that the head does not reach to the top of the grid. Check against the illustration to make sure you copy the design accurately. Then go over the final drawing with your black felt marker.

PUNCHING THE DESIGN

Purple (3) *Long loop:* Punch one row across the top of the head. Punch two rows above and two rows below the zigzag area of the teeth. Outline and fill in the arms along either side of the body. Punch one row all along the bottom of the body, then outline and fill in the four triangles just above it. Outline and fill in the two sides of the vest and the inverted triangle in the middle of the bottom of the vest.

Green (4) *Short loop:* Fill the upper part of the head but leave the eyes bare for the moment. Fill in the chin area. Fill in the two sides of the body and the two triangles in the center at the bottom of the vest. Punch the lower zigzag line of the teeth.

Lemon yellow (2) *Short loop:* Fill in the lower part of the eyes. Punch the upper zigzag line of the teeth. Outline and fill in the hands at the bottom of each arm. Fill in the second, fourth and sixth horizontal stripes in the vest, and the second and fourth vertical stripes at the bottom of the body.

Hot pink (1) *Short loop:* Fill in the upper part of the eyes. Fill in the background area around the zigzag lines of the teeth. Fill in the first, third and fifth horizontal stripes in the vest, and the first, third and fifth vertical stripes at the bottom of the body.

Check for any skimpy spots and fill in if necessary.

See Chapter 11 for instructions for trimming your pillow, and Chapter 12 for finishing it.

Moe

MATERIALS

Burlap: 16″ × 18″ (tape the edges)
Yarn: yellow orange, 25 yards
　　　green, 37 yards
　　　red orange, 15 yards
　　　wine, 23 yards

TRIM

1 bright brass curtain ring (with or without a knob)

FOR FINISHING

Iron-on interfacing: 14″ × 16″
Backing: 16″ × 18″
Stuffing: ½ pound polyester fiber

TRANSFERRING THE DESIGN

Leave a 2-inch margin on all sides and draw a grid of 2-inch squares, 6 squares wide by 7 squares high, with your blue felt marker.

Locate the peak of the head and the beak as key points on your grid. Note that the rounded sides of the body do not quite reach the edges of the grid. The dotted-line circles indicate the placement of the brass curtain ring—you don't have to draw them on your burlap. Use a ruler to draw all the straight lines. Copy the rest of the design, square by square, from the illustration. Go over the final drawing with your black felt marker.

PUNCHING THE DESIGN

Wine (4) *Long loop:* Outline the beak. Outline and fill in the triangles at each end of the hat, and the two triangular wings at the sides of the body.

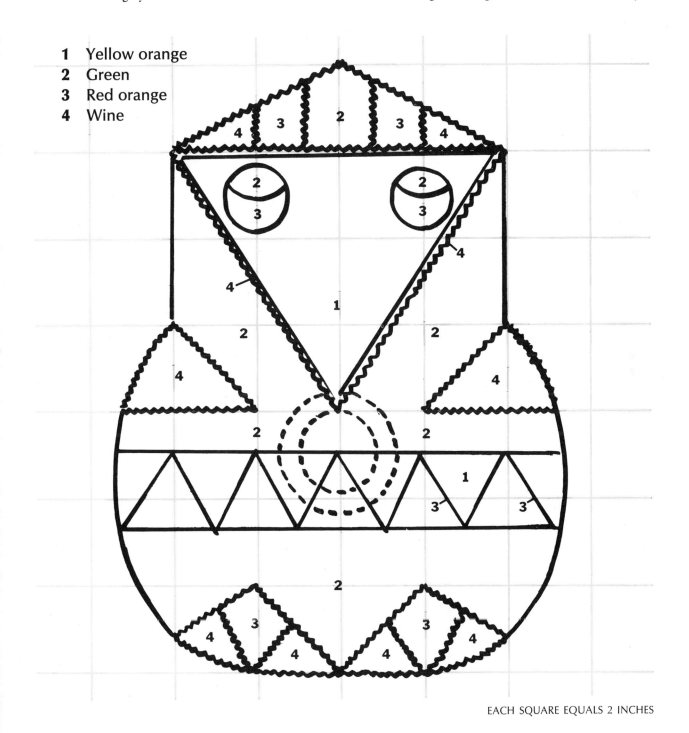

1 Yellow orange
2 Green
3 Red orange
4 Wine

EACH SQUARE EQUALS 2 INCHES

Outline and fill in the four triangles in the feet at the bottom of the body.

Green (2) *Long loop:* Fill in the center area of the hat. *Short loop:* Fill in the upper area of the eyes. Outline and fill in the upper part of the head and body above the horizontal band across the center. Then outline and fill in the area of the body below the horizontal center band and above the feet.

Red orange (3) *Long loop:* Fill in the two re-maining areas of the hat and the center areas in both feet. *Short loop:* Punch the zigzag line across the center band. Fill in the lower part of the eyes.

Yellow orange (1) *Short loop:* Fill in the beak. Fill in the area around the zigzag line of the center band.

Check for any skimpy spots and fill in if necessary.

See Chapter 11 for instructions for trimming your pillow, and Chapter 12 for finishing it.

Max

MATERIALS

Burlap: 14″ × 20″ (tape the edges)
Yarn: purple, 20 yards
      lemon yellow, 25 yards
      red orange, 30 yards
      wine, 35 yards

TRIM

2 bright brass curtain rings (with or without knobs)

FOR FINISHING

Iron-on interfacing: 12″ × 18″
Backing: 14″ × 20″
Stuffing: ½ pound polyester fiber

TRANSFERRING THE DESIGN

Leave a 2-inch margin on all sides and draw a grid of 2-inch squares, 5 squares wide by 8 squares high, with your blue felt marker.

Locate the triangle above the eyes, the triangular feet and the zigzag centerline as key points on your grid. The dotted-line circles indicate the placement of the brass curtain rings—you don't have to draw them on your burlap. Except for the eyes, you can draw the entire design on your grid with a ruler.

Check against the illustration to make sure you copy it accurately. Then go over the final drawing with your black felt marker.

PUNCHING THE DESIGN

Wine (4) *Short loop:* Outline and fill in the diagonal band on either side of the head. Fill in the center of the eyes. Outline and fill in the area of the body around the horizontal stripes in the center.

Purple (1) *Long loop:* Punch one row across the top and one row across the bottom of the zigzag line of the teeth. *Short loop:* Outline and fill in the lower part of the eyes. Punch the zigzag line of the teeth. Outline and fill in the third and sixth stripes in the center of the body.

Red orange (3) *Long loop:* Outline and fill in the two ear triangles at the top corners of the head, and the two feet triangles at the bottom corners of the body. *Short loop:* Outline and fill in the area of the head around the eyes, above the upper purple horizontal line. Fill in the first and fourth stripes in the center of the body.

Lemon yellow (2) *Long loop:* Fill in the large triangle in the center of the head above the eyes. *Short loop:* Fill in the second and fifth stripes in the center of the body. Fill in the background area around the purple zigzag line.

Check for any skimpy spots and fill in if necessary.

See Chapter 11 for instructions for trimming your pillow, and Chapter 12 for finishing it.

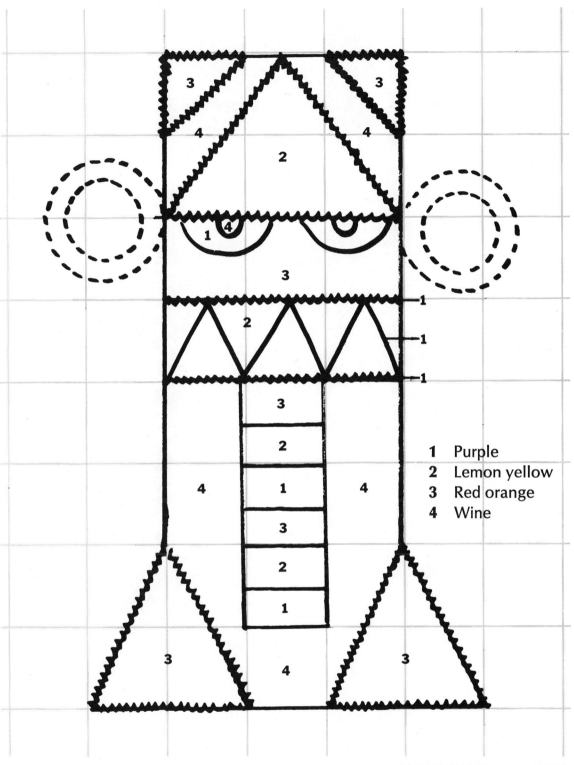

1 Purple
2 Lemon yellow
3 Red orange
4 Wine

EACH SQUARE EQUALS 2 INCHES

CHAPTER

9

THE GARDEN

You can turn your couch into an indoor garden of sorts—the kind that never needs weeding or watering—by punching a flower garden bolster such as the one in this chapter. Add some daisy pillows (see Chapter 4) to make it even more luxuriant, and enliven it with butterflies, snails and insects—the kind you never have to worry about spraying.

There's a house and barn landscape bolster for you to make, too, that looks particularly attractive on a window seat. Instead of using backing and stuffing, the punched design for this and the flower garden were hand-sewn onto ready-made covered foam-rubber bolsters. However, if you have a bolster of a different size or shape that you want to re-cover, you can adapt the dimensions of either design to fit it.

Both bolsters can be punched without a frame, but the size of the burlap makes them a bit bulky to handle. If you think you'd find it easier to work with a frame, see page 23 for additional information.

The Small Butterfly

MATERIALS

Burlap: 12″ × 16″ (tape the edges)
Yarn: black, 25 yards
     gold, 9 yards
     rust, 9 yards
     cream, 15 yards
     turquoise, 8 yards

FOR FINISHING

Iron-on interfacing: 10″ × 14″
Backing: 12″ × 16″
Stuffing: ¼ pound polyester fiber

TRANSFERRING THE DESIGN

Leave a 2-inch margin on all sides and draw a grid of 2-inch squares, 4 squares high by 6 squares wide with your blue felt marker.

Locate the top and bottom of the body, and the line dividing the upper wings from the lower wings as key points on your grid. Copy the rest of the design, square by square, from the illustration. The solid black areas in the illustration indicate black yarn is to be used—you don't have to blacken them on your burlap. Go over the final drawing with your black felt marker.

PUNCHING THE DESIGN

Black (1) *Long loop:* Outline the entire butterfly, including the body. Fill in the black areas in the upper wings and in the lower part of the body. Punch the dividing lines between the upper and lower wings. Punch the two rows that run diagonally across the lower wings from the midline down. Punch the three horizontal lines across the upper part of the body.

Rust (3) *Short loop:* Fill in the upper part of the body between the horizontal black rows. Outline and fill in the two triangular areas in the center of the upper wings. Outline the two circles in the upper wings. Outline and fill in the two circles in the lower wings, near the body. Outline and fill in the two areas in the bottom of the lower wings.

Turquoise (5) *Short loop:* Fill in the circles in the upper wings. Outline and fill in the triangles on either side of the body in the upper wings. Outline and fill in the areas on either side of the body in the lower wings, around the small rust circles. Outline and fill in the two circles on the upper outer edge of the lower wings.

Gold (2) *Short loop:* Outline and fill in the two middle areas in the upper wings. Outline and fill in the outer areas in the lower wings around the two turquoise circles.

Cream (4) *Short loop:* Fill in the areas in the upper wings around the rust-outlined turquoise circles. Fill in the two middle areas in the lower wings.

Check for any skimpy spots and fill in if necessary.

See Chapter 12 for instructions for finishing your pillow.

EACH SQUARE EQUALS 2 INCHES

1 Black
2 Gold
3 Rust
4 Cream
5 Turquoise

The Big Fat Butterfly

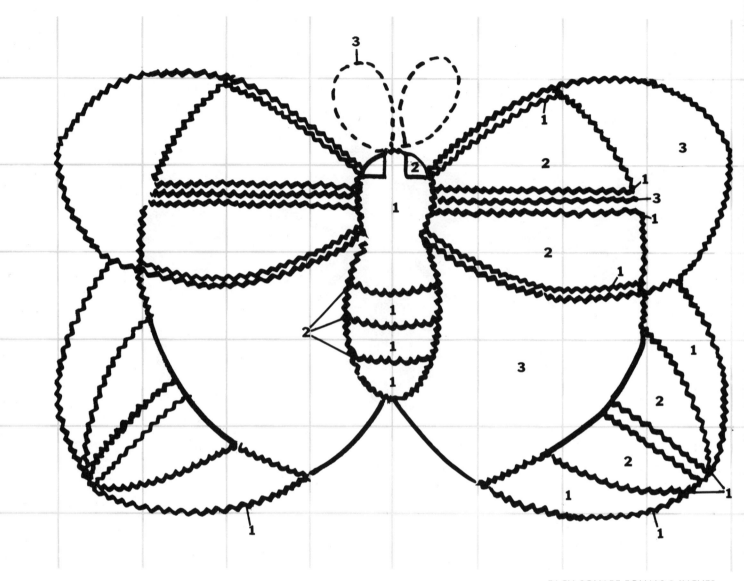

EACH SQUARE EQUALS 2 INCHES

1 Black
2 Red
3 Purple

MATERIALS

Burlap: 14″ × 20″ (tape the edges)
Yarn: black, 55 yards
  red, 30 yards
  purple, 55 yards

TRIM

Purple yarn antennae

FOR FINISHING

Iron-on interfacing: 12″ × 18″
Backing: 14″ × 20″
Stuffing: ¾ pound polyester fiber

TRANSFERRING THE DESIGN

Leave a 2-inch margin on all sides and draw a grid of 2-inch squares, 5 squares high by 8 squares wide, with your blue felt marker.

Locate the top and bottom of the body and the dividing line between the upper and lower wings as key points on your grid. Copy the rest of the design, square by square, from the illustration. The dotted lines are for the antennae—you don't have to draw them on your burlap. Go over the final drawing with your black felt marker.

PUNCHING THE DESIGN

Purple (3) *Long loop:* Outline and fill in the tips of the two upper wings. Punch one line across the center of the inner sections of the upper wings. *Short loop:* Outline and fill in the two inner sections of the lower wings.

Black (1) *Long loop:* Outline the body and fill it in, but leave three rows bare for the red stripes. Punch two rows at the top and two rows at the bottom of the inner section of the upper wings. Punch one row on either side of the purple row across the center of the upper wings. Outline the lower wing tips. Fill in the two side areas of the lower wing tips, and punch two rows across the center of each.

Red (2) *Long loop:* Punch the three horizontal lines across the lower part of the body. *Short loop:* Fill in the two inner sections of the upper wings. Fill in the two inside sections in the lower wing tips. Punch the eyes.

Check for any skimpy spots and fill in if necessary.

See Chapter 11 for instructions for trimming your pillow, and Chapter 12 for finishing it.

The Snail

MATERIALS

Burlap: 14″ × 18″ (tape the edges)
Yarn: purple, 20 yards
      lavender, 18 yards
      gold, 16 yards
      maroon, 16 yards
      gray, 12 yards

TRIM

purple yarn antennae
2 small round maroon buttons for the antennae

FOR FINISHING

Iron-on interfacing: 12″ × 16″
Backing: 14″ × 18″
Stuffing: ½ pound polyester fiber

TRANSFERRING THE DESIGN

Leave a 2-inch margin on all sides and draw a grid of 2-inch squares, 7 squares wide by 5 squares high, with your blue felt marker.

Locate the curved lines of the snail's body at the bottom of the design and the dot in the center of the swirl of the shell as key points on your grid. Copy the snail's body first. (The antennae are not punched but are part of the trim—there's no need to draw them on your burlap.) Then starting at the central dot, draw a curving line spiraling outward for the shell. To divide the shell into color sections, start at the bottom and work in toward the center. The dotted lines represent single rows of color that are different from the color of the sections around them. Check against the illustration to be sure you've copied the design accurately. Go over the final drawing with your black felt marker.

PUNCHING THE DESIGN

(NOTE: *The entire design is punched in short loop.*)

Gold (3): Punch the dot at the center of the swirl of the shell. Continue from there and punch the outline of the swirl of the shell until you reach the snail's head at the bottom. Then outline and fill in the body at the base of the design.

Purple (1): Outline and fill in the bottom section of the shell, just above the body. Find the other three sections of the shell keyed for purple and fill them in.

Maroon (4): Outline and fill in the section just above the bottom purple section of the shell. Find the other three sections of the shell keyed for maroon and fill them in, but leave a row bare where the dotted line indicates.

Lavender (2): Proceeding upward, outline and fill in the section of the shell just above the bottom maroon section, but leave one row bare for the dotted line between the two sections. Find the other four sections of the shell keyed for lavender and fill them in, but leave bare the row indicated by the dotted line next to the section keyed for gray.

Gray (5): Outline and fill in the section just above the lavender, but leave two rows bare in the middle. Find the other three sections keyed for gray and fill them in, but leave bare any rows indicated by dotted lines.

NOTE: The dotted lines are to be punched in different colors. If you have any scraps of colored yarn that will blend with this color scheme, such as taupe, old rose, rust or wine, use them to punch the dotted lines. If you have no such scraps, use maroon in or next to the gray section, and purple in or next to the maroon sections.

Check for any skimpy spots and fill in if necessary.

See Chapter 11 for instructions for trimming your pillow, and Chapter 12 for finishing it.

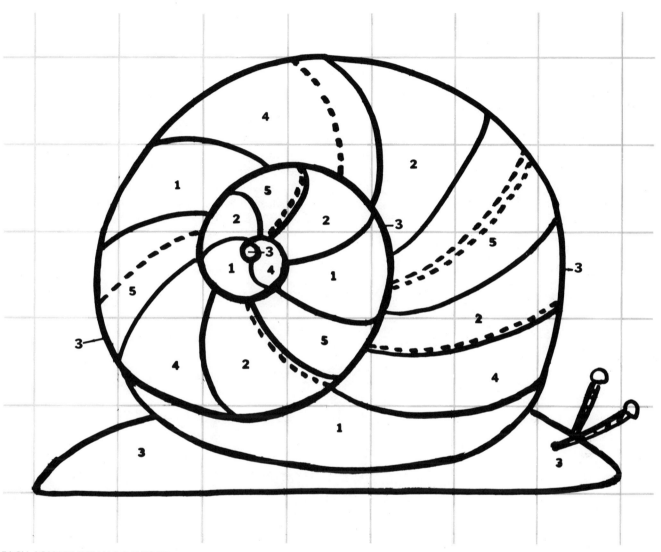

EACH SQUARE EQUALS 2 INCHES

1 Purple
2 Lavender
3 Gold
4 Maroon
5 Gray

Green Tomato Caterpillow

MATERIALS

Burlap: green, 12″ × 32″ (tape the edges)
Yarn: dark olive, 48 yards
    emerald green, 50 yards
    grass green, 50 yards
    chartreuse, 38 yards
    pale yellow, 20 yards
    red orange, 35 yards

TRIM

2 round chartreuse eye buttons
pale yellow yarn antennae

FOR FINISHING

Iron-on interfacing: 10″ × 30″
Backing: Red orange, 7″ × 36″
Stuffing: ¾ pound polyester fiber

1   Dark olive
2   Emerald green
3   Grass green
4   Chartreuse
5   Pale yellow
6   Red orange

TRANSFERRING THE DESIGN

Leave a 2-inch margin on all sides and draw a grid of 2-inch squares, 4 squares wide by 14 squares long, with your blue felt marker.

Locate the two ovals on the centerline as key points on your grid. Note that the head, the tail and each body section is two squares long by four squares wide. The curved lines going down through each segment are also uniform in size and shape except at the tail, where the inside curve arches in the opposite direction. Copy the design, section by section, from the illustration. Go over the final drawing with your black felt marker.

PUNCHING THE DESIGN

Red orange (6) *Long loop:* Punch one row across the top of the head. *Short loop:* Fill in the center of the eyes. Fill in the ovals in the center of the head and the center of the tail. Fill in the ovals in each section of the body. Connect each oval in the body to the one beside it with two rows of punches.

Dark olive (1) *Long loop:* Starting from the top corner of the head, punch the line that curves down and in toward the side of the center oval on both sides of the head. Punch one row around the red orange eyes. Punch the six horizontal lines separating each section of the body, and the line at the bottom of the tail. Then punch one row along each of the two curved lines that outline the inner side of the ovals in the body. When you reach the tail, continue with the reversed curved line in the tail. *Short loop:* Outline the two sides of the Caterpillow, starting just below the curved lines of long loop olive down to the bottom of the tail.

Pale yellow (5) *Long loop:* Punch one row around the eyes just outside of the dark olive out-line. Outline the oval in the center of the head and the oval in the center of the tail. Punch one row down the center of the back to the tail section.

Emerald green (2) *Short loop:* Fill in the area in the head around the eyes. Fill in the area between the outer edge and the first curved line along both sides of the body and both sides of the tail section.

Grass green (3) *Short loop:* Fill in the curved band on the outer side of each of the red ovals in the body. Fill in the curved band next to the dark olive row that outlines the inner side of each of the red ovals in the body. Fill in the band on either side of the dark olive row in both parts of the tail section.

Chartreuse (4) *Short loop:* Fill in the back area of the head. Fill in the area on either side of the pale yellow centerline all the way down the body. Fill in the area in the tail on either side of the yellow-outlined center oval.

Check for any skimpy spots and fill in if necessary.

See Chapter 11 for instructions for trimming your pillow, and Chapter 12 for finishing it.

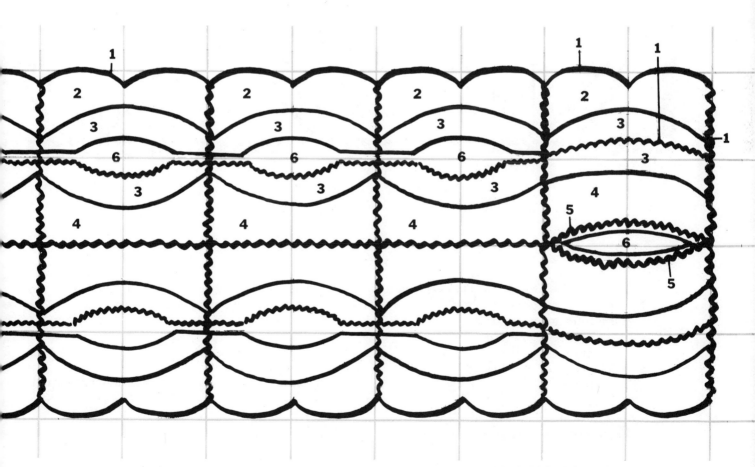

EACH SQUARE EQUALS 2 INCHES

The Flower-Garden Bolster

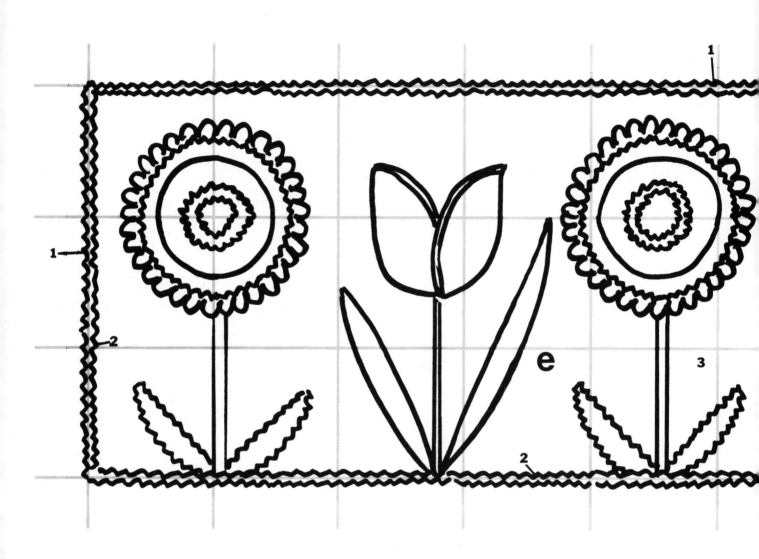

MATERIALS

Burlap: 42″ × 18″, or 6 inches longer and wider than the size of your bolster (tape the edges)

Yarn: forest green, 60 yards
    chartreuse, 60 yards
    olive, 170 yards
    yellow orange, 40 yards
    brown, 30 yards
    red orange, 35 yards
    lemon yellow, 30 yards

Frame (optional): inside opening, 38″ × 16″

FOR FINISHING

Iron-on interfacing: 39″ × 15″, or 3 inches shorter and narrower than the size of your burlap

Backing ⎫
Stuffing ⎭ See note below.

Note: In place of backing and stuffing, a standard-sized foam-rubber bolster, 36″ × 12″ × 9″, was purchased at Sears Roebuck, together with a corduroy zip-on cover. The covers come in several

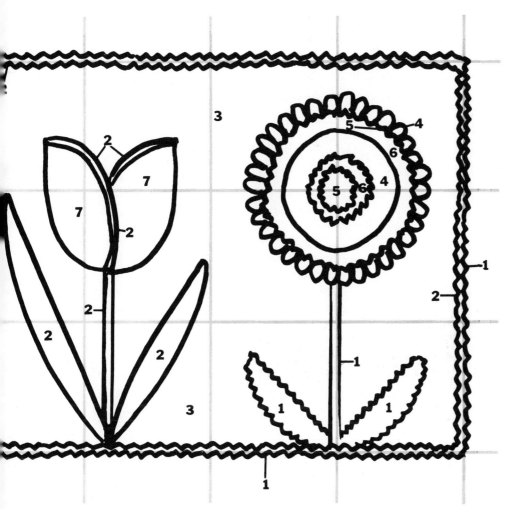

1 Forest green
2 Chartreuse
3 Olive
4 Yellow orange
5 Brown
6 Red orange
7 Lemon yellow

EACH SQUARE EQUALS 4 INCHES

colors. For this bolster, an avocado-colored corduroy cover was chosen which closely matches the olive yarn used for the background.

TRANSFERRING THE DESIGN

(Because this design is so large, the grid used is made of 4-inch squares instead of the 2-inch squares used for most of the other pillows, and a 3-inch rather than a 2-inch margin is provided to make it easier to use a frame.)

Leave a 3-inch margin on all sides and draw a grid of 4-inch squares, 9 squares wide by 3 squares high, with your blue felt marker.

Locate the three round flowers first as key points on your grid. The stems of the two flowers at either end follow the lines of the grid; the third flower is exactly in the center of the design. Center the tulips midway between the round flowers. Check against the illustration to make sure you've copied the design accurately, then go over the final drawing with your black felt marker.

PUNCHING THE DESIGN

Forest green (1) *Long loop:* Punch one row around for the outside margin. Outline and fill in the leaves on either side of each of the three round flowers. *Short loop:* Punch three rows to make the stem of each round flower.

Chartreuse (2) *Long loop:* Punch one row around the margin just inside the forest green. *Short loop:* Outline and fill in the leaves on either side of the two tulips. Punch two rows to make the stem of each tulip, and one row for the line up the center and across the top of each tulip flower.

THE ROUND FLOWERS

The easiest way to punch these is to start at the center and work out. Begin with

Brown (5) *Long loop:* Fill in the center of each flower.

Red Orange (6) *Long loop:* Punch one row around the brown center.

Yellow orange (4) *Short loop:* Punch five rows around the red orange.

Red orange (6) *Long loop:* Punch two rows around the yellow orange.

Brown (5) *Long loop:* Punch one row around the red orange.

Yellow orange (4) *Extra long loop* (see page 28): Punch one row around to complete each flower.

Olive (3) *Short loop:* Fill in the background.

Lemon yellow (7) *Short loop:* Fill in the tulip petals.

Check for any skimpy spots and fill in if necessary.

See Chapter 12 for instructions for finishing your bolster.

VARIATIONS

You can change the arrangement or the colors of the flowers in any way you choose. To adapt the flower garden to fit a bolster of a different size, measure the length and width of the bolster you want to re-cover and add 6 inches to each dimension to determine the size of the burlap you'll need. If you don't have a ready-made cover in a color that goes with your garden, buy a piece of material to use for backing in a solid color that matches the background of your design. Be sure you buy it large enough, then tailor it to fit.

House and Barn Landscape Bolster

MATERIALS

Burlap: 42″ × 18″, or 6 inches longer and wider than the size of your bolster (tape the edges)
Yarn: grass green, 100 yards
    royal blue, 85 yards
    red, 45 yards
    forest green, 50 yards
    white, 50 yards
    purple, 35 yards
    brown, 8 yards
Frame (optional): inside opening, 38″ × 16″

TRIM

4 or 5 round red buttons for apples
1 small white button for a doorknob

FOR FINISHING

Iron-on interfacing: 39″ × 15″, or 3 inches shorter and narrower than the size of your burlap
Backing } See note below.
Stuffing

NOTE: In place of backing and stuffing, a standard-sized foam-rubber bolster, 36″ × 12″ × 9″, was purchased at Sears Roebuck, together with a corduroy zip-on cover. The covers come in several colors. For this bolster, a royal blue cover was chosen which closely matches the yarn used for the sky.

TRANSFERRING THE DESIGN

(Because this design is so large, the grid is made of 4-inch squares instead of the 2-inch squares used for most of the other pillows, and a 3-inch rather than a 2-inch margin is provided to make it easier to use a frame.)

Leave a 3-inch margin on all sides and draw a grid of 4-inch squares, 9 squares wide by 3 squares high, with your blue felt marker.

Locate the house and barn first as key points on your grid. Then draw the overlapping trees, the grass, the clouds and the horizon. Check against the illustration to make sure you've copied the design accurately. Go over the final drawing with your black felt marker.

PUNCHING THE DESIGN

Grass green (1) *Long loop:* Outline the entire design. Punch three additional rows across the bottom for the grass. Outline and fill in the tops of the two round trees.

Forest green (4) *Long loop:* Outline and fill in the two Christmas trees.

Brown (7) *Short loop:* Outline and fill in the trunks of the round trees.

Red (3) *Short loop:* Fill in the barn, but leave the roof and the outline and crossbars of the door bare for the moment. Punch the roof, the chimney and the door of the house. Punch one row to outline the window.

Purple (6) *Short loop:* Outline and fill in the hills in the background. Punch the roof of the barn. Turn your burlap over. Working from the front, outline and fill in the small triangular window in the house. Still working from the front, fill in the center band in the large window.

Royal blue (2) *Short loop:* Fill in the whole sky, except for the clouds. Turn your burlap over. Working from the front, fill in the two bands in the window on either side of the purple.

White (5) *Short loop:* Punch the outline and the crossbars of the barn door. Fill in the clouds. Fill in the house.

Check for any skimpy spots and fill in if necessary.

See Chapter 11 for instructions for trimming your bolster, and Chapter 12 for finishing it.

VARIATIONS

You can change the colors or the design of the trees or the house and barn in any way you choose. To adapt the house and barn landscape to fit a bolster of a different size, measure the length and width of the bolster you want to re-cover and add 6 inches to each dimension to determine the size of the burlap you'll need. If you don't have a ready-made cover in a color that harmonizes with your landscape, buy a piece of material to use for backing in a solid color that matches the background of your design. Be sure you buy it large enough, then tailor it to fit.

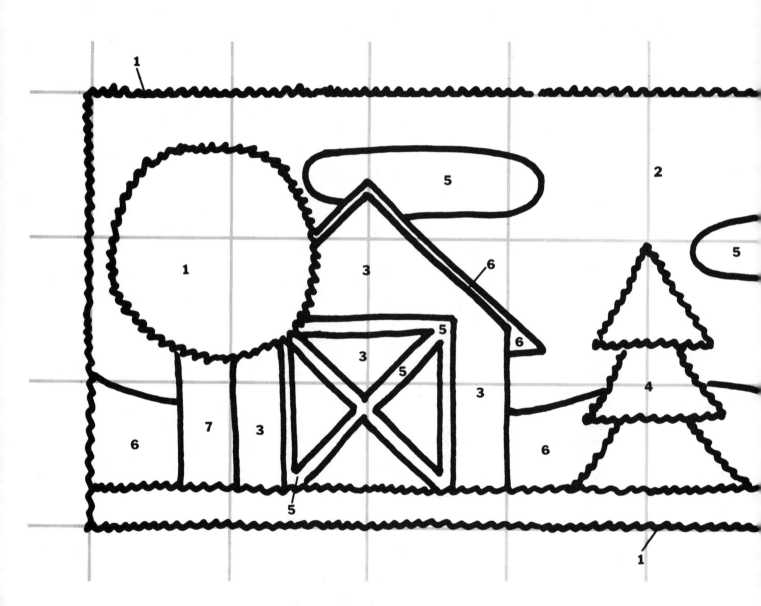

1 Grass green
2 Royal blue   5 White
3 Red   6 Purple
4 Forest green   7 Brown

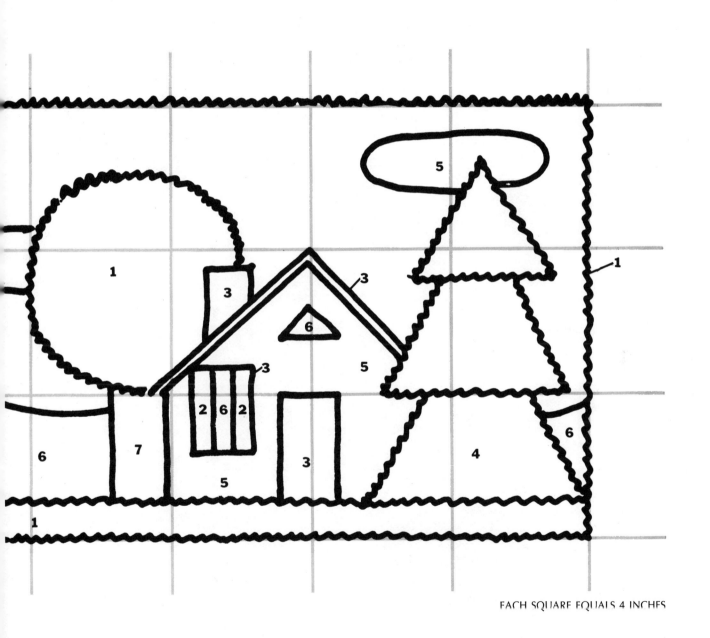

EACH SQUARE EQUALS 4 INCHES

CHAPTER

10

CHRISTMAS STOCKINGS AND BIRD TAPESTRIES

Christmas stockings make welcome gifts. In Europe, children set out their shoes on Christmas Eve for St. Nicholas to fill. The stocking designs given here incorporate that Old World tradition —they come equipped with shoes.

All three stockings are the same size, which should help insure peace on Christmas morning if you're making them for more than one youngster in a family. They're all quite easy to make, too, and you can punch them at any time of the year and tuck them away until Christmas time arrives.

The bird tapestries can be punched as individual pictures and hung separately, or sewn together to make a larger single hanging. If you'd prefer to see them as pillows on your couch rather than pictures on your wall, you can back them and stuff them just as you do any of the punch pillows. Similarly, you can turn any of the pillow designs into a tapestry by adding a background, if necessary, to make it a square or a rectangle, and then following the instructions given on page 159.

Christmas Stockings

Because all three stockings are the same size and shape, the easiest way to proceed is to make a cardboard pattern of the outline of the stocking. You can then use it over and over again to make as many stockings as you wish.

On a piece of cardboard at least 12″ × 16″, draw a grid of 2-inch squares, 5 squares wide by 7 squares high, with your black felt marker. Copy the outline of one of the stockings onto your grid. Do not include any of the details. Check against the illustration to make sure you've copied it accurately, then cut out the cardboard stocking shape.

Dimensions are given with each design, but you can turn any piece of burlap into a Christmas stocking as long as it's big enough to allow you at least a 2-inch margin on all sides after you've traced the stocking outline onto it. You can even trace two (or more) stockings onto the same piece of burlap if there's room enough. Flip the cardboard over to make one facing toward the right and one toward

the left—that way they'll be able to toe in on either side of the fireplace.

TRANSFERRING THE DESIGN

This applies to all three stocking designs. Use the cardboard outline and trace the outline of the stocking onto your burlap with your blue felt marker. Copy the details of the particular design you want to make onto your burlap stocking from the illustration. Check the grid lines on your cardboard stocking against the grid lines in the illustration to see where the tops of shoes or stripes begin, and then locate them on your burlap. Use a ruler to draw the horizontal stripes. Check against the illustration to make sure you've copied all the details accurately, then go over the final drawing with your black felt marker.

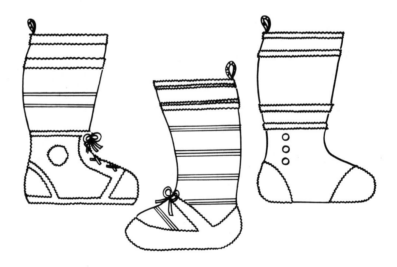

The Sneaker

EACH SQUARE EQUALS 2 INCHES

MATERIALS

Burlap: red, 14″ × 18″ (tape the edges)
Yarn: forest green, 10 yards
    chartreuse, 15 yards
    red, 5 yards
    white, 10 yards

TRIM

1 chartreuse yarn shoelace
1 chartreuse yarn hang loop

FOR FINISHING

Iron-on interfacing: 12″ × 16″
Backing: red or green, 14″ × 18″

PUNCHING THE DESIGN

Chartreuse (2) *Long loop:* Punch three rows across for each of the two bands in the upper part of the stocking. Outline and fill in the toe and heel patches of the sneaker. *Short loop:* Punch one row across for each of the narrow bands in the lower half of the stocking.

Red (3) *Long loop:* Outline and fill in the circle in the center of the sneaker. *Short loop:* Fill in the narrow area between the two narrow bands of chartreuse in the lower half of the stocking.

Forest green (1) *Long loop:* Outline and fill in the center of the sneaker around the red circle.

White (4) *Long loop:* Punch two rows across the top of the sneaker and two rows across the bottom. Fill in the bands separating the heel and the toe from the center with two rows each. Then punch three rows for the band down the front. (The shoelaces will be added later as trim—there's no need to leave spaces for them.) *Short loop:* Fill in the narrow area between the two chartreuse bands in the upper half of the stocking.

Check for any skimpy spots and fill in if necessary.

See Chapter 11 for instructions for trimming your sneaker, and Chapter 12 for finishing it.

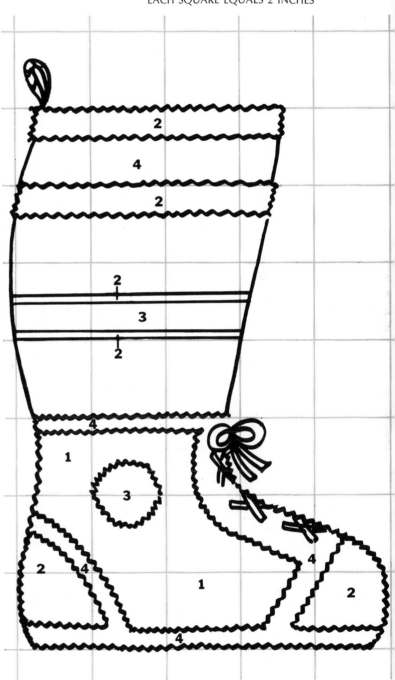

1 Forest green
2 Chartreuse
3 Red
4 White

The Mary Jane

MATERIALS

Burlap: green, 14″ × 18″ (tape the edges)
Yarn: black, 10 yards
    red, 10 yards
    chartreuse, 10 yards
    pink, 10 yards

TRIM

1 black yarn bow
1 red yarn hang loop

EACH SQUARE EQUALS
2 INCHES

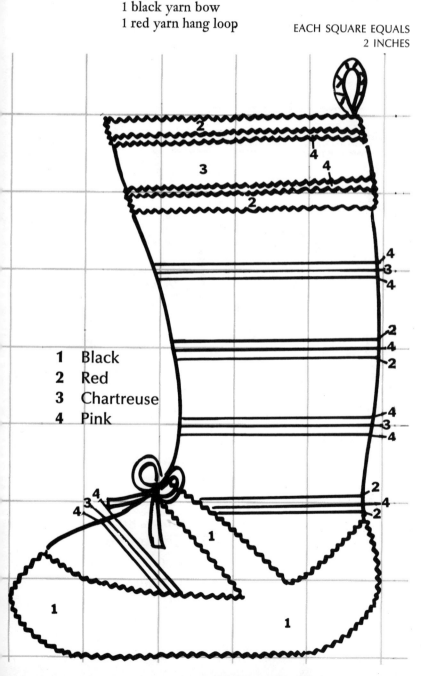

1 Black
2 Red
3 Chartreuse
4 Pink

FOR FINISHING

Iron-on interfacing: 12″ × 16″
Backing: red or green, 14″ × 18″

PUNCHING THE DESIGN

The easiest way to punch this stocking is to start at the top and work down.

THE UPPER PART OF THE STOCKING

Red (2) *Long loop:* Punch two rows across the top.

Pink (4) *Long loop:* Punch one row across just underneath the red.

Chartreuse (3) *Short loop:* Fill in the area below the pink, above the second band.

Pink (4) *Long loop:* Punch one row across for the top of the second band.

Red (2) *Long loop:* Punch two rows across just beneath the pink.

THE NARROW BANDS

These are all punched in short loop and alternate as follows:

First band: One row of pink, one row of chartreuse and one row of pink.

Second band: One row of red, one row of pink and one row of red.

Third band: Same as first.

Fourth band: Same as second.

Fifth band: Same as first.

THE SHOE

Black (1) *Long loop:* Outline and fill in the shoe. Make the shoestrap 3 rows wide. (The bow will be added later as trim—there's no need to leave any spaces for it.)

Check for any skimpy spots and fill in if necessary.

See Chapter 11 for instructions for trimming your stocking, and Chapter 12 for finishing it.

The Spat

MATERIALS

Burlap: white, 14″ × 18″ (tape the edges)
Yarn: forest green, 10 yards
    grass green, 15 yards
    red, 5 yards
    black, 11 yards

TRIM

3 round red buttons
1 forest green yarn hang loop

FOR FINISHING

Iron-on interfacing: 12″ × 16″
Backing: red or green, 14″ × 18″

PUNCHING THE DESIGN

Forest green (1) *Long loop:* Punch two rows across for each of the four narrow bands.

Red (3) *Short loop:* Fill in the narrow area between the two bands in the upper part of the stocking. Then fill in the narrow area between the two bands in the lower part.

Grass green (2) *Short loop:* Fill in the center of the stocking.

Black (4) *Long loop:* Fill in the heel and the toe of the shoe. The three little circles indicate button placement. (The spat is created by the white burlap left bare.)

Check for any skimpy spots and fill in if necessary.

See Chapter 11 for instructions for trimming your stocking, and Chapter 12 for finishing it.

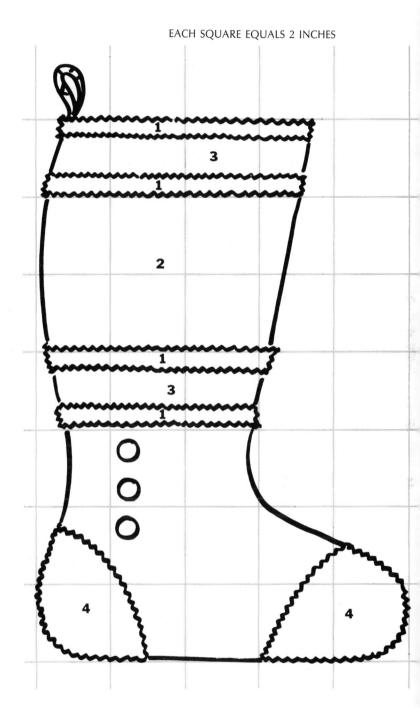

1 Forest green
2 Grass green
3 Red
4 Black

Bird Tapestries
The Woodpecker

MATERIALS

Burlap: blue, green or turquoise, 12″ × 14″ (tape the edges)
Yarn: black, 10 yards
      red, 10 yards
      yellow orange, 2 yards
      brown, 14 yards
      white, 6 yards

TRIM

1 small black eye button
2 ⅝-inch dowels
1 red yarn double-twist hang cord

FOR FINISHING

Iron-on interfacing: 12″ × 14″
Backing (optional): 12″ × 14″

TRANSFERRING THE DESIGN

Leave a 2-inch margin on all sides and draw a grid of 2-inch squares, 4 squares wide by 5 squares high, with your blue felt marker.

Locate the eye, the wings and the tail as key points on your grid. Copy the rest of the design, square by square, from the illustration. The solid black areas on the design indicate black yarn is to be used—you don't have to blacken them on your burlap. Go over the final drawing with your black felt marker.

PUNCHING THE DESIGN

(NOTE: *The entire design is punched in short loop.*)

Red (2): Punch the outside border. Outline and fill in the head.

Black (1): Punch one row around just inside the red border. Outline and fill in the wings, but leave the two white areas bare for the moment. Outline and fill in the tail, except for the white area.

Yellow orange (3): Punch one row for each toe line. Outline and fill in the beak, tapering to one row where it touches the tree.

Brown (4): Outline and fill in the tree trunk including the area between the toes.

White (5): Outline and fill in the body. Fill in the white spots on the wings and the tail.

Check for any skimpy spots and fill in if necessary.

See Chapter 11 for instructions for trimming your tapestry, and Chapter 12 for finishing it.

EACH SQUARE EQUALS 2 INCHES

1 Black
2 Red
3 Yellow orange
4 Brown
5 White

The Cardinal

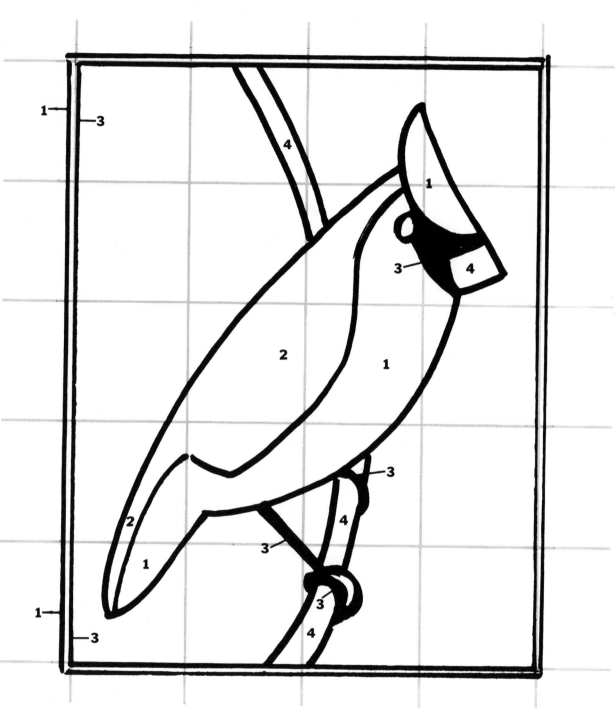

EACH SQUARE EQUALS 2 INCHES

1 Bright red
2 Dark red
3 Black
4 Yellow orange

MATERIALS

Burlap: blue, green or turquoise, 12″ × 14″ (tape the edges)
Yarn: bright red, 13 yards
     dark red, 6 yards
     black, 5 yards
     yellow orange, 2 yards

TRIM

1 small black eye button
2 ⅝-inch dowels
1 red yarn double-twist hang cord

FOR FINISHING

Iron-on interfacing: 12″ × 14″
Backing (optional): 12″ × 14″

TRANSFERRING THE DESIGN

Leave a 2-inch margin on all sides and draw a grid of 2-inch squares, 4 squares wide by 5 squares high, with your blue felt marker.

Locate the top knot, the beak and the tail as key points on your grid. Copy the rest of the design, square by square, from the illustration. The solid black areas on the design indicate black yarn is to be used—you don't have to blacken them on your burlap. Go over the final drawing with your black felt marker.

PUNCHING THE DESIGN

(NOTE: *The entire design is punched in short loop.*)

Bright red (1): Punch one row around for the outside border. Outline and fill in the top of the head. Outline and fill in the belly and the lower part of the tail.

Black (3): Punch one row around just inside the red border. Fill in the black area of the face. Punch the legs and toes.

Dark red (2): Outline and fill in the back and upper part of the tail.

Yellow orange (4): Punch two rows to make the branch above and below the bird. Outline and fill in the beak.

Check for any skimpy spots and fill in if necessary.

See Chapter 11 for instructions for trimming your tapestry, and Chapter 12 for finishing it.

The Gold Finch

MATERIALS

Burlap: blue, green or turquoise, 12″ × 14″ (tape the edges)
Yarn: black, 16 yards
lemon yellow, 12 yards
yellow orange, 3 yards
white, 2 yards
chartreuse, 5 yards

TRIM

1 small black eye button
2 ⅜-inch dowels
1 black yarn double-twist hang cord

FOR FINISHING

Iron-on interfacing: 12″ × 14″
Backing (optional): 12″ × 14″

TRANSFERRING THE DESIGN

Leave a 2-inch margin on all sides and draw a grid of 2-inch squares, 5 squares wide by 4 squares high, with your blue felt marker.

Locate the head, the tail and the wing as key points on your grid. Copy the rest of the design, square by square, from the illustration. The solid black areas indicate black yarn is to be used—you don't have to blacken them on your burlap. Go over the final drawing with your black felt marker.

PUNCHING THE DESIGN

(NOTE: *The entire design is punched in short loop.*)

Black (1): Punch one row around for the outside border. Outline and fill in the black area on the head. Outline and fill in the wings and the tail, but leave the white areas bare for the moment. Punch the branch, making it three rows wide below the bird's feet and two rows wide above his body. Don't punch the toe area.

Chartreuse (5): Punch one row around just inside the black border.

Yellow orange (3): Outline and fill in the beak. Then punch one row to outline the belly from the beak to the wing, and one row to outline the back of the head. Fill in the toes.

Lemon yellow (2): Fill in the body.

White (4): Fill in the white areas in the wings and the tail.

Check for any skimpy spots and fill in if necessary.

See Chapter 11 for instructions for trimming your tapestry, and Chapter 12 for finishing it.

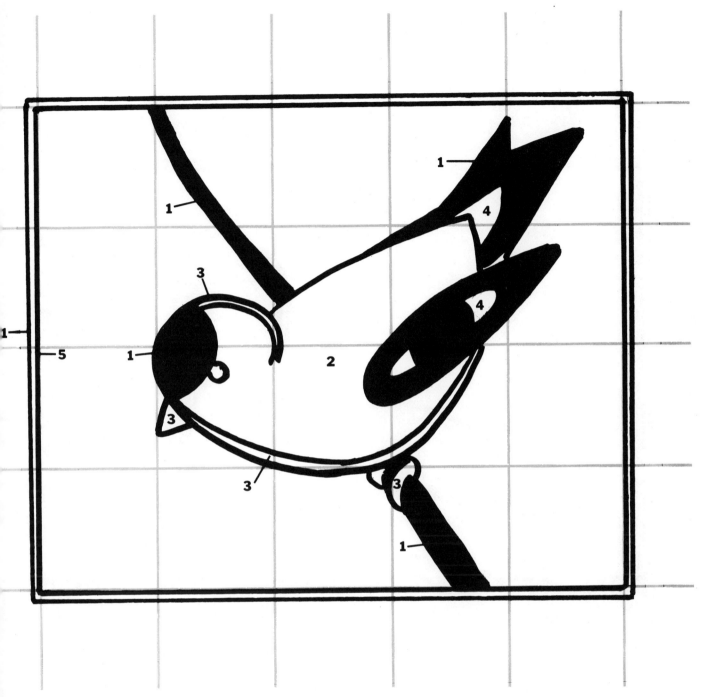

EACH SQUARE EQUALS 2 INCHES

1 Black
2 Lemon yellow
3 Yellow orange
4 White
5 Chartreuse

The Ruddy Duck

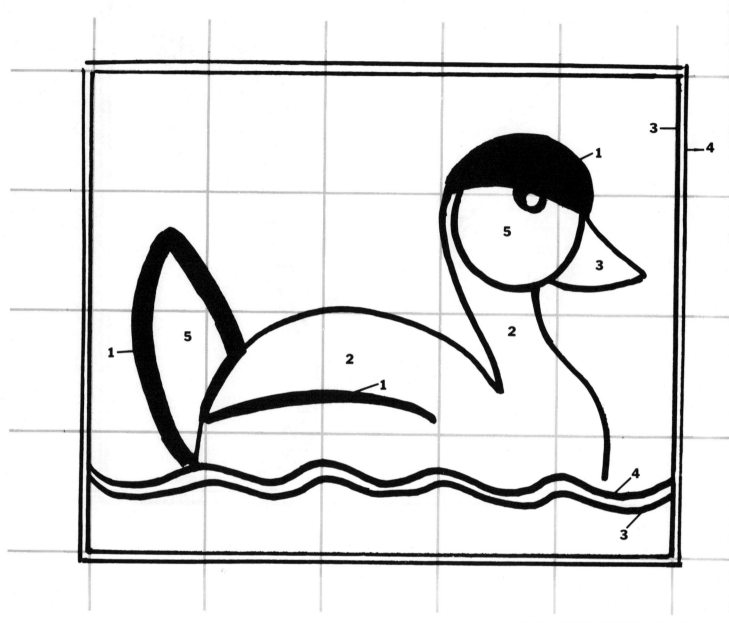

EACH SQUARE EQUALS 2 INCHES

1 Black
2 Rust
3 Blue
4 Dark green
5 White

MATERIALS

Burlap: blue, green or turquoise, 12″ × 14″ (tape the edges)
Yarn: black, 5 yards
     rust, 15 yards
     blue, 7 yards
     dark green, 5 yards
     white, 5 yards

TRIM

1 small black eye button
2 ⅝-inch dowels
1 black yarn double-twist hang cord

FOR FINISHING

Iron-on interfacing: 12″ × 14″
Backing (optional): 12″ × 14″

TRANSFERRING THE DESIGN

Leave a 2-inch margin on all sides and draw a grid of 2-inch squares, 5 squares wide by 4 squares high, with your blue felt marker.

Locate the black cap, the bill, the curve of the back and the tail as key points on your grid. Copy the rest of the design, square by square, from the illustration. The solid black areas on the design indicate black yarn is to be used—you don't have to blacken them on your burlap. Go over the final drawing with your black felt marker.

PUNCHING THE DESIGN

(NOTE: *The entire design is punched in short loop.*)

Dark green (4): Punch one row around for the outside border. Punch the top wavy line of the water.

Blue (3): Punch one row around just inside the dark green border. Punch the lower wavy line of the water. Outline and fill in the beak.

Black (1): Outline and fill in the black area on the top of the head. Punch one row for the line of the wing, and two rows to outline the tail.

Rust (2): Outline the neck and body and fill in.

White (5): Fill in the face and tail.

Check for any skimpy spots and fill in if necessary.

See Chapter 11 for instructions for trimming your tapestry, and Chapter 12 for finishing it.

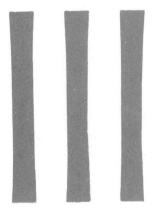

PART

III

How to Finish

CHAPTER

11

TRIMMING YOUR PILLOW

HERE ARE THE TRIMMINGS I used to decorate the punch pillows and tapestries described in the preceding chapters. Read the instructions carefully. In some cases you'll have to refer to the next chapter to learn how to finish your pillow, in part or entirely, before you can complete the trim.

All kinds of odds and ends can be used to trim your pillows. Don't let yourself be limited by the ones I've used. Use your imagination, together with whatever scraps of yarn, buttons and bows, ribbons and junk jewelry you can find to make your pillows uniquely yours.

USING YARN AS TRIM

The whiskers, shoelaces, bows, antennae, tongues and tails that add the finishing touches to many of the pillows are all made of yarn. The yarn required to trim each pillow is listed under "Trim" at the beginning of the particular design. Yarn is used in single strands, double strands, or it is braided or twisted to achieve different effects. Except where noted otherwise, yarn trim is added after the design is completely punched and before the interfacing is ironed on.

Single or Double Strands for Whiskers and Shoelaces

Although you can use your punch needle to punch in single strands of yarn for trim, it's easier to use an upholstery needle with a large eye.

To make punched single-strand whiskers or bows (Baby, Little Sister, Little Brother, the Cat), thread your needle and punch it through the burlap from the back to the front. Draw the loose end of the yarn out on the right side, about four inches. Make another punch close to the first, pull the yarn out to the same length and cut it on the right side. Tie the ends together to make a bow, or leave them untied for whiskers. If you are making whiskers, repeat the procedure on the opposite side of the face. Trim the ends to the desired length. Then apply hot candle wax or Elmer's Glue to the ends of the yarn to keep them from fraying and to stiffen the whiskers.

To make single-strand shoelaces (Father, the Sneaker Stocking), thread your upholstery needle and stitch it through from front to back. Leave the loose end of the yarn out on the right side. Stitch the number of X's indicated in the illustration in a zigzag fashion so that you end with your yarn on top alongside the starting strand. Cut the yarn on the right side and tie the two ends together in a bow. Trim them if necessary, and apply hot candle wax or Elmer's Glue to keep them from fraying.

To make double-strand whiskers (the Lion), thread your punch needle with two separate strands of worsted yarn, then follow the procedure described for making punched single-strand whiskers.

Braids for Shoe Bows, Antennae, Snake Tongues and Hang Loops

Braids can be made separately and then sewn onto the punched burlap, or they can be made right on the burlap with your punch needle. Whichever kind you're making, keep in mind that braiding shortens the yarn, and allow yourself enough yarn to account for that shortening. If you're not sure how much yarn to start with, make a practice braid the length you want it to be, undo it and use that yarn length as a guide.

To make a braided shoe bow (the Mary Jane Stocking), take three pieces of yarn, knot them together at one end, braid them and knot the other end. Make the braid into a bow, then stitch the center of it onto the burlap where indicated in the design.

To make separate antennae (the Big Fat Butterfly, the Caterpillow). After the backing is sewed on and the pillow is stuffed, take three 18-inch strands of yarn, knot them at one end, braid them together and knot the other end. Form the braid into two loops by tying it in the middle with a piece of thread. Sew the dividing point between the loops onto the center of the seam at the top of the head. Insert one knot into an opening in the seam just to the right of the center, the other knot into an opening in the seam just to the left. Stitch both seam openings closed.

To make punched antennae (the Snail). Use your punch needle set for long loop. Thread it and punch through the burlap from the back to the front so that your needle comes out at the point indicated in the design. Pull out the loose end of the yarn on the right side about 2½ inches. Skip two rows and punch through again, pulling out the loop to the same 2½ inch length. Go back to the first punch, punch another loop and pull it out to the same length. Return to the second punch, push the needle through, pull out the yarn to the same length and cut it on the right side. Cut each of the loops in half. This will give you three strands of yarn of equal length for each antenna. Make two separate braids and knot each one at the end. Sew a button onto the end of each braid, looping the thread around the end of the braid to hold it securely. Apply hot candle wax or Elmer's Glue to the antennae to keep the yarn from fraying and to stiffen them.

To make a snake's tongue (the Rattlesnake).

SNAKE'S TONGUE

Take six 8-inch strands of yarn, tie a knot in one end, divide the strands into three groups of two strands each, and braid them until you have a braid 2½ inches long. At that point, separate the six strands into two groups of three strands each, and make two separate, narrower braids for the forked tongue. Knot each braid at the end and trim if necessary. The snake's tongue is not inserted until after the interfacing is ironed on, the tail is completed, the body is stuffed and you are stitching the backing for the head in place. Insert the back of the tongue between the front of the mouth and the backing. Then stitch the seam closed, leaving the front of the tongue hanging out.

To make a hang loop (the Christmas Stockings). After the stocking is completely finished, take three strands of yarn the same color as the top band of the stocking, knot them together at one end and make a braid about three inches long. Knot the other end, form the braid into a loop, insert the two ends inside an opening in the seam at the top of the stocking at the back, and stitch the seam closed.

Double Twists for Hair Bows, Tails and Hang Cords

Double-twisted yarn can be used as trim in many ways—to add to the character of a punch pillow, as a border around its edges or to hang a tapestry. It can even serve as a strap for a shoulder bag if you decide to turn one of your pillows into a bag instead of stuffing it.

Double twists are always made the same way, although they can be made with more than two strands of yarn if you want to make an especially thick cord. You can use three or even four strands if you like. And instead of using all of them in the same color, you can use different colored yarns to achieve a multicolored effect. The length, too, is up to you, although if you try to use strands that are too long, you may have to stand on a ladder when you're suspending your twist with the scissors dangling in the middle.

To make a double twist. Take two strands of yarn of equal length, twice the length you want the finished twist to be. Knot them together at one end. Hook that end over a nail or ask a friend to hold it for you. Hold the yarn taut at the opposite end and twist it to the right until the entire length is twisted tightly. Still holding your end firmly, slip a scissors handle over the twisted strands and let it dangle in the middle. Then take both ends of the yarn in one hand and hold them up high. The scissors dangling in the middle will spin, double-twisting the yarn. Stop the scissors from spinning as soon as it begins to turn in the opposite direction. With another pair of scissors or a knife, cut the yarn in the middle to free the scissors, but hold onto the new ends so that the yarn doesn't begin to untwist. Knot both ends of the double-twisted strands.

To make a double-twisted hair bow (Little Black Sister). Take two strands of yarn, each 1½ yards long, knot them together at one end and double-twist them as described above. Make the double-twisted yarn into a bow. After the pillow is completely finished, sew the bow onto the top of the head where indicated in the illustration.

To make a double-twisted tail (the Mouse). Take two strands of yarn, each 1 yard long, knot them together at one end and double-twist them as described above. When you sew on the backing for the mouse, leave an opening in the seam at the back, directly opposite the nose. Insert one end of the tail into the opening, then stitch the seam closed.

To make a double-twisted hang cord (Bird Tapestries). After your tapestry is completely finished and the dowel is inserted, take two strands of yarn, 1¼ yards each, and double-twist them as described above. If the dowel protrudes at the sides of the tapestry, knot one end of the cord around the dowel on either side. If the dowel does not protrude, stitch one end at each side of the back of the tapestry, at the top. (NOTE: If you attach two tapestries together horizontally and plan to hang them that way, double the length of the yarn you use to make a long enough double-twist hang cord.)

BUTTONS

Buttons bring a pillow to life. They provide the details that add interest to a scene or a character, and the features that put a spark of life into the people and animals.

The buttons required for each pillow are listed under "Trim" at the beginning of the particular design. You may use different colors or shapes if you choose, but it's important to keep the sizes in proportion to the size of the subject they're adorning, and in proportion to each other if more than one button is used on a pillow. After all, you don't want the apples to be as big as the tree, or the eyes to be smaller than the belly button.

For Eyes

All the people pillows except Father, and most of the animals, birds, fish and monsters are trimmed with eye buttons. If you don't want to use the buttons suggested for a particular design, pick a color and size that seem appropriate for the face you're trimming. In most cases shiny buttons are preferable—a shiny button adds a gleam to the eye.

For Noses

All the people pillows and one or two of the others have nose buttons. The types of buttons suited for noses are more limited than those suited for eyes. The most useful, all-purpose nose button I've found is a small pink pearl one. (The same pink pearl button makes the best belly button.) A leather button makes a good nose for a dog, especially if you use slightly smaller, matching leather buttons for the eyes. If your pillow is made of colored burlap, it's generally a good idea to try to match the color of the nose button to the burlap "skin." But final choice of a nose button, as with eye buttons, depends on the personality of the pillow creature.

For Details

I used a diamond button for Uncle Dudley's stickpin; gold buttons for his waistcoat, Girl Rider's jacket and as trim on the Belly Dancer's costume; pink pearl buttons for belly buttons for Little Brother and the Belly Dancer; white pearl buttons on Little Black Sister's spats, the Mermaid's breasts and for the doorknob in the House and Barn bolster; a heart-shaped button for the Mermaid's mouth; and round red buttons for the apples in the House and Barn bolster and the spat on the Christmas stocking. You may use any buttons you like for decorative details on your pillows, as variations on the designs included here or on designs of your own

making. For example, attractive buttons of varied shapes and colors can be worked in very effectively as part of an abstract design on a square or triangular punched pillow.

Attaching the Buttons

Check the illustration to see where to locate the buttons for the particular design you've punched, then use a needle and heavy duty thread to sew each button in place. However, *do not attach any buttons until after the interfacing is ironed on to the back of the punched design.* Buttons make bumps which complicate the ironing. Also, the addition of the interfacing provides a firmer foundation to hold the buttons.

CURTAIN RINGS

Plain brass or colored plastic curtain rings are used for eyeglasses for Big Brother, earrings for Big Sister and Girl Rider, and as trim for the three Little Creatures from Outer Space. Ordinary washers may be substituted for the curtain rings if you prefer.

Attaching the Rings

As with the buttons, these are stitched onto the punch pillows with a needle and heavy duty thread.

Big Brother's glasses are fitted on around his eye buttons after the interfacing is ironed on and his eye buttons are sewn in place. Each ring is then secured at both sides and at the top.

The earrings on Big Sister and Girl Rider are attached on either side of the face, as indicated by the dotted lines in the illustrations. Manny's rings are attached at the top of his head, Moe's ring at the point of his beak and Max's rings at the sides of his head, as shown in those illustrations. However, *before you sew on any of these rings, iron on the interfacing and finish the pillows completely.* Stitch the earrings on Big Sister and Girl Rider only at the top so that they can dangle freely. For the three little space creatures, you can use curtain rings that have knob eyelets if they're available. If you do, fit each knob into an opening in the seam where the dotted line indicates the ring belongs, and then stitch it in place. If the rings have no knobs, just sew each one firmly onto the seam on the outside so that it's held fairly rigidly.

MISCELLANEOUS TRIM

After the interfacing is ironed on and your pillow is backed and stuffed, you can enhance its appearance in a number of different ways. You can sew on striped ribbon to make suspenders for a pair of pants, flowered ribbon to decorate the band of a skirt, or you can stitch on a ribbon hair bow or a head band. You can pin an old campaign button, a Scout medal, a school award or an Army ribbon onto one of your punch people to add to his or her character. Or you can use beads for trim by stringing them together and stitching them in place. I used chain, ribbon, fringe and a baby's rattle to achieve certain effects for some of the pillow people and animals. Here's how to do that.

Completing the Other Trim

To make Uncle Dudley's watch chain, drape a piece of narrow gold chain across his waistcoat as shown in the illustration. Stitch it at both ends and let it dangle in the middle.

To make a winner's award for Girl Rider, take a piece of blue satin ribbon, one-half or one-quarter inch wide, and fold it into a rosette as shown in the drawing. Sew a gold button in the center. Then sew the rosette onto Girl Rider's jacket, or pin it on with a little gold safety pin.

To give the lion his mane, finish him completely, but leave a small opening in the seam at each ear when you stitch on the backing. Tuck one end of the upholstery fringe into the opening at one ear and run the fringe across the top of his head to the other opening. Cut the fringe, but leave enough to tuck into the second seam opening. Use a needle and heavy duty thread to sew the fringe in place. Take another piece of fringe, tuck the end into one of the seams and run it around the bottom of the lion's head, under his cheeks and up the other side. Cut the fringe, again leaving enough to tuck into the second opening. Stitch this piece of fringe in place, then sew both seam openings closed. Finally, sew a small piece of upholstery fringe around the tip of the lion's tail.

To complete the Rattlesnake's tail. After you have ironed on the interfacing, lay the punched burlap down on a table, wrong side up. Place the baby's rattle at the end of the tail. Wrap the punched rattle part of the design around it so that the right side is showing. Fold the margins in and sew that part of the body together, enclosing the rattle. (NOTE: The Rattlesnake is too long and narrow to sew up inside out, so it is finished on the right side.) If you can't find a baby's rattle for your snake, put a handful of gravel or dried beans into a small, empty frozen-juice can and use that as a substitute.

CHAPTER

12

FINISHING

THERE ARE CERTAIN DIFFERENCES involved, depending on whether you are finishing a pillow, a bolster cover, a Christmas stocking or a tapestry, but the first few steps are the same for all.

You have punched the entire design, and you have checked it over and filled in any of the spots that looked a little bare. Use a knitting needle to even up any of the loops that seem to need it. Then take your scissors and trim any loose ends of yarn that need to be shortened to match the height of the loops around them.

If your design is to be trimmed, look at Chapter 11 to see whether the trim should be added before the interfacing is ironed on or after. Buttons are always sewed on after the interfacing has been added. Yarn trim, if it is punched on, is added before the interfacing; if it is made separately, it's usually not attached until after the pillow is almost completely finished. So check the instructions carefully for the particular trim your design requires.

THE IRON-ON INTERFACING

Iron-on interfacing is applied to the back of all punched designs to keep the loops from pulling out and to reinforce the burlap. It's available wherever yard goods are sold, and comes in both a woven and an unwoven form. Either one will serve your purpose, although the woven kind gives the burlap more body. Be sure to buy iron-on interfacing that is *fusible on one side only*.

Ironing on the Interfacing

Put the punched burlap, wrong side up, on an ironing board and place the interfacing, sticky side down, on top of it. Be sure the interfacing covers 1″ of the margin on all sides as well as the entire back of the design. (Note: If you are finishing a tapestry, the iron-on interfacing is the same size as the burlap and should cover the entire back plus the whole margin.) Iron on the interfacing according to the directions on the package. Iron the margins separately to make sure that the interfacing adheres to them completely as well as to the rest of the design—it will strengthen the area you'll be sewing and prevent your seams from fraying later on. Let the fabric cool before proceeding with the finishing.

THE BACKING

Both the punch pillows and the Christmas stockings need backing. If your bolster cover is to be sewn onto a ready-made cover, you don't have to worry about backing it. And if you are making a tapestry, it can be finished with or without backing—backing simply gives it a more finished look and helps it keep its shape longer.

The material you use for backing should be a sturdy cloth in a solid color that matches one of the major colors in your design. Dark colors are more practical than light ones. If your design is punched in white, yellow and blue, for example, it's best to try to find a matching blue cloth to use as backing. Corduroy, bark cloth, denim, linen and cotton velveteen all make good backing materials.

Pinning on the Backing

After the interfacing is ironed on, pin (or baste) the backing in place. Lay the punched design, right side up, on a table and place the backing, right side down, on top of it. With your fingers, push up the loops along the edges of the design. Then run your fingernail along the edge of the backing to crease it down to the base of the pushed-up loops. Pin the backing to the burlap close to the base of the loops.

If you are making a pillow, pin the backing on all the way around but leave a large enough opening at the bottom or on one side so you can turn it right side out, and through which you can insert the stuffing.

If you are making a Christmas stocking, pin the backing on all the way around the sides and the bottom, but leave the top open with enough extra material so that you can hem it and the burlap later.

If you are backing a tapestry, pin the cloth on all the way around but leave enough of an opening to turn it right side out, plus a small opening on each side at the top for the dowel to be inserted.

Sewing on the Backing

Sew the backing on either by hand or machine. If you are sewing by hand, use a tight running stitch close to the base of the loops and avoid catching any of the loops in your stitches. If you're sewing by machine, stitch with the backing side up. Use the pressure foot running alongside the loops to keep them standing up straight as you sew in close to the loops' base. Be sure you don't sew closed any of the openings you need. Remove the pins or basting stitches when you're finished.

Trimming the Seams

Trim the backing and the burlap together. Leave about a half-inch allowance beyond the seams and a slightly wider allowance along the edges of any openings. Clip or notch the seam allowance where necessary. Clip angles wherever the seam takes a new direction, and seams curve in. Notch seams that curve out.

Turn your pillow or stocking right side out. If a seam pulls, turn it inside out again and make an additional clip or notch wherever it's needed.

THE STUFFING

Polyester fiber makes the best pillow stuffing. It's soft, nonallergenic, doesn't bunch or shift, is easy to handle and doesn't fly all over the room while you're working with it. Shredded foam rubber can be used instead, but it's somewhat lumpier and messier to work with. Old nylon stockings, if you have any on hand, can also be used as stuffing material.

Stuffing Your Pillow

Take the stuffing, a handful at a time, and push it well into the corners of your pillow. Stuff all corners—all toes, ears and tails—before filling in the larger areas. If your hand is too large, use a ruler or the end of a pencil to poke the stuffing in where you want it. Continue adding handfuls of stuffing until the entire pillow is taut. Then, when you think your pillow is fully stuffed, add a few more handfuls. Punch pillows, with the exception of the Rattlesnake and the Caterpillow look much better when they are tightly packed.

Closing the Gap

When your pillow is stuffed as tightly as possible, fold in the edges of the backing and the burlap and pin the gap closed. Sew it closed by hand, using matching thread and an overcast stitch. Remove the pins and punch the pillow a few times to settle the stuffing.

FINISHING THE RATTLESNAKE AND THE CATERPILLOW

The method of backing and stuffing these two punch pillows varies somewhat from the others because of their character and their shape.

The Rattlesnake

The Rattlesnake is too long and narrow to finish inside out, so it is finished on the right side. The punched burlap tail is wrapped around the baby's rattle and stitched closed first, as described on page 154. Once that is done, continue to progress forward, folding in the margins and sewing the body closed, little by little. Use an overcast stitch and stuff the body with polyester pellets as you go along. Do not stuff the snake too tightly—you want him to be slinky rather than rigid when you're through.

When you reach the middle of the first big diamond, add the cloth backing for the head. Fold the edges in and pin the backing in place with the narrow end pointing toward the tail. Sew the back and sides of the backing in place first, stuffing as you sew. Before you finally close the front, insert the tongue as described on page 152. Then finish stuffing the head and sew the opening closed.

The Caterpillow

The backing for the Caterpillow is actually his bottom or underside, and it is both longer and narrower than the burlap. Lay the backing flat on a table, right side up. Take the punched burlap, right side down, and arch it over the backing in a tunnel shape, as shown in the illustration. Pin the backing

and the burlap together along each side. Turn the backing up at each end and baste it to the edges of the burlap in the form of an arch. The Caterpillow should measure five inches across from side to side and four inches high when you're finished.

Sew the backing and the burlap together at both ends and each side, but leave an opening about eight inches wide along one side toward the middle of the body. Trim the seams to half an inch and turn the Caterpillow right side out. Stuff him through the opening in the side, but don't stuff him too firmly—he should be more squashy than the other pillows. Sew the opening closed by hand with an overcast stitch. See page 152 for instructions for adding the antennae.

FINISHING A CHRISTMAS STOCKING

With the interfacing ironed onto the burlap and the backing sewed on to both sides and the bottom, turn the top of the backing and burlap over and hem them to the wrong side of the stocking. When you're finished, turn the stocking right side out and iron it lightly from the back if it seems to need it. Add the hang loop (see page 152 for instructions for making one) by stitching it onto the top of the back of the stocking as directed, and your stocking is ready to hang up for Santa Claus.

FINISHING A BOLSTER

After you've ironed on the interfacing, take your scissors and trim the burlap until it is the same size as the interfacing—39″ × 15″. Fold the margins under and sew the punched cover by hand to the ready-made cover on your bolster.

FINISHING A TAPESTRY

Once you've ironed on the interfacing and sewed on the eye button, the tapestry can be finished with or without backing.

Without Backing

Leave a one-inch burlap border around your punched picture and fold the rest of the margins to the back—the sides first, then the top and bottom. Tuck the taped edge under as you pin the margins in place. Hem each margin carefully to the back of the burlap so that the stitches don't show through. Leave a large enough opening on both sides of the top and bottom hems for the dowels to be inserted.

If you prefer, instead of sewing the hems, you may seal them closed with iron-on mending tape. If you use this method, omit tucking under the taped edges.

With Backing

For a more finished look, add a solid color backing to your tapestry in a matching shade. Pin the backing to the punched burlap, right side to right side. Sew it closed all around but leave two small openings in the side seams at the top for the dowel to be inserted, and enough of an opening in the bottom so that you can turn the tapestry right side out. Trim the seams, turn the tapestry to the right side and stitch the bottom closed.

Getting the Tapestry Ready to Hang

The ⅜-inch dowels you use to hang your tapestry may be cut to the same width as the tapestry or allowed to protrude slightly at each side. Insert one dowel through the opening at one side of the top and the other through an opening at the side of the bottom, and secure them in place either by stapling or sewing them in with a needle and thread so they can't slip. If the dowel ends protrude, color them with a felt marker to harmonize with the tapestry background.

Using yarn that repeats one or more of the colors in the design, make a double-twisted hang cord (see page 153 for instructions). If the dowel ends do not protrude, sew one end of the cord to each side of the back of the tapestry at the top. If they do protrude, tie one end of the cord to each end of the dowel.

You may hang your bird tapestries in pairs – the Woodpecker with the Cardinal, the Gold Finch with the Ruddy Duck. To hang them vertically, use black yarn and an upholstery needle to stitch the bottom of one tapestry to the top of the other. To hang them horizontally, put the two of them, facing toward each other, on a single dowel long enough to hold them both and double the amount of yarn you use to make a double-twisted cord to hang them.